The Louisville Review

Number 90
Fall 2021

The Louisville Review

TLR publishes two volumes each year: spring and fall. Visit our website for complete guidelines, back issues, subscriptions, and more: www.louisvillereview.org.

Like us on Facebook for up to date information about each issue, news on contributors, etc.: www.facebook.com/TheLouisvilleReview. Follow us on Twitter @TheLouRev.

Questions? Our please note our email and mailing addresses:

managingeditor@louisvillereview.org.

The Louisville Review Corp.
1436 St. James Court #1
Louisville, Kentucky 40208

This issue: $10 ppd
Sample copy: $5 ppd
Subscriptions: One year, $18; two years, $36; three years, $54 plus $2 shipping.
Foreign subscribers, please add $35/year for shipping.

The text and the cover printed in the United States. Cover design by Jonathan Weinert. Cover artwork, Corie Neumayer, *Sunday Morning*, acrylic and latex on canvas, 24 x 30 inches. Photo by Ron Schildknecht.

The Kentucky Arts Council, the state arts agency, provides American Rescue Plan funds to The Louisville Review Corporation with federal funding from the National Endowment of the Arts. *The Louisville Review* is a not-for-profit publication.

The Louisville Review Corporation is a member of the Community of Literary Magazines and Presses.

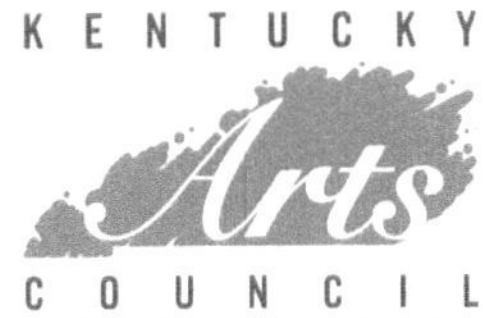

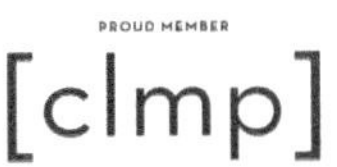

Associate Editor's Note

With this issue, we celebrate the forty-fifth anniversary of *The Louisville Review*! First, I must express our deep gratitude to the individuals and organizations that have supported *TLR*. Next, I'm delighted to announce that, thanks to the efforts of Managing Editor Amy Foos Kapoor, this fall *TLR* is the recipient of a one-time grant from the Kentucky Arts Council that greatly contributes to our ability to publish the journal, now fully independent again after generous university sponsorship over past years: first from the University of Louisville and then from Spalding University.

Founded by Editor Sena Jeter Naslund, along with two undergraduate students at the University of Louisville, *TLR* has continuously published both new and established writers since 1976. We wish to thank Frederick Smock and Nathan Gower for serving as Guest Poetry Editor and Guest Fiction Editor for this issue. For this special anniversary issue #90, our cover features new work by painter Corie Neumayer, *Sunday Morning*. With colors evoking sunlight filtered through a geometry of clean lines, *Sunday Morning* suggests a bright, distinctly urban landscape. To my eye, it's a painting that gestures toward a specifically *human* world that is complex, very much alive, and that invites exploration.

In the spirit of embracing that complex—and international—world, we open this issue with a suite of poems spanning multiple nations and times by Regina Derieva (1949-2013), both in the original Russian text and in English translation by Frederick Smock. These poems appear from *Images in Black, Continuous*, Smock's recently published collection of Derieva's poems in translation from M-Graphics Publishing. This issue also includes fiction that explores the convergence of multiple worlds and times: in Nadeem Zaman's "The Holy Visit," an immigrant family from Pakistan living in Chicago wrestles with the loss of a son in their adopted home in the U.S.—while still haunted by family deaths in Pakistan's war of liberation in 1971.

Continuing *TLR*'s commitment to the interrelatedness of the arts, in #90 we feature a nonfiction essay by Neumayer to accompany her painting. Neumayer describes how the ongoing pandemic has, for her, called for new ways of seeing that led to embracing new aesthetic approaches. The theme of looking at the world differently—or looking at a different world—due to constraints of the pandemic emerges also in Kelly Craig's short story, "We Cook a Family Meal," and in poems by Olga-Maria Cruz, inspired by quarantine use of Window-Swap, a website where visitors can experience the views of strangers through webcams that look out of windows across the globe.

"I Couldn't Say No," an excerpt from poet Jonathan Weinert's recently completed memoir, *Five Minutes in Heaven*, articulates another kind of struggle and resilience in the face of emotional isolation: Weinert's searing prose portrays a childhood, and a life, complicated by a mother's ambiguous psychological abuse.

Deepening our engagement at *TLR* with music as well as visual art, this issue includes Sarah Gorham's " 'Benedictus,' *Requiem*, by Wolfgang Amadeus Mozart." Gorham's essay meditates on sensual and intellectual joys of music spanning adolescence to adulthood and also narrates her experience attending a rehearsal of Mozart's *Requiem* performed by the Louisville Orchestra, led by conductor Teddy Abrams.

In this issue, Amy Foos Kapoor and I very much enjoyed editing our section of poetry by writers in grades K-12, *Cornerstone*. I'd like to list and thank our guest editors who, along with myself, Amy Foos Kapoor, and Editor Sena Jeter Naslund in fiction, have selected the poetry and fiction for this forty-fifth anniversary issue of *The Louisville Review*. With great appreciation for your work:

Nathan Gower holds an MFA in fiction writing from Spalding University and a PhD in humanities with emphasis in aesthetics and creativity from the University of Louisville. His work has been published in *Baltimore Review, Birmingham Arts Journal, Louisville Magazine, Louisville Review, New Southerner, Santa Fe Literary Review, Valparaiso Fiction Review* and elsewhere. He currently serves as Associate Professor of English at Campbellsville University. His work is represented by literary agent and foreign rights manager Danielle Bukowski of Sterling Lord Literistic.

Amy Foos Kapoor is the managing editor of *The Louisville Review*, and a writer, television/digital media producer, and event coordinator for the annual summer reading series, "Voice & Vision: Presented by Spalding University's School of Writing, *The Louisville Review*, and 21c Museum Hotel" in Louisville, Kentucky. She earned an MFA from Spalding University, where she studied writing for children & young adults.

Frederick Smock is professor of English at Bellarmine University. He served as 2017-18 Kentucky poet laureate. His books include The *Blue Hour* (Larkspur Press) and *The Bounteous World* (Broadstone Books), and he has published in such journals as *The Southern Review, The Hudson Review, The Iowa Review*, and others.

—Flora K. Schildknecht, Associate Editor

Table of Contents

Poetry

Non-fiction

Fiction

Cornerstone

work by writers K-12

Poetry

Regina Derieva

Сочинение на заданную тему

Обмакни палец в огонь
и твори Вселенную.
Сосед приходит из школы
и говорит: «Что тебе стоит
написать за меня сочинение,
от него будет зависеть
моя годовая оценка...»
А у меня палец в огне,
который вот-вот может
погаснуть, может остыть,
и не будет
уже никогда Вселенной,
а будет только
сочинение на тему
«Творчество
и его применение в жизни».

Regina Derieva

Composition on a Given Theme

Dip a finger in the fire
and create the universe.
Someone comes from the school
and says, "That costs you nothing,
so, write me a composition.
Your annual grade
will depend on it."

But I have my finger in fire,
which can
go out, can cool down,
and after that will never be the universe
but only
this poor composition on the theme,
"Creativity
and its application in life."

Translated from the Russian by Frederick Smock

Regina Derieva

Научный зоопарк

Нас заставляли читать
труды В. И. Ленина.
Многие завидовали тому,
что мы их читаем
в подлиннике и бесплатно.
Не так ли и в зоопарке?
Многие завидуют
волкам и прочим, полагая,
что тем не надо думать
о завтрашнем дне.

Regina Derieva

Scientific Zoo

We were forced to read
works by V. I. Lenin,
leader of scientific communism.
Many people abroad were jealous
of the fact
that we read him
in the original and free-of-charge.
Is it not the same in a zoo?
Many are jealous of
wolves and other beasts,
believing that
they do not have to think
about sustenance and the near future.

Translated from the Russian by Frederick Smock

Regina Derieva

Со вторых рук

Носить одежду со вторых рук
легко и удобно; ты за нее
как бы не отвечаешь, поскольку
у нее уже был хозяин,
поступавший с ней, как хотел.
В конце концов, она вышла
из моды, но нашелся тот,
кого устроила цена,
и он ударил с одеждой по рукам.
С прежним запахом и прежним
настроением, она, в сущности, умерла,
но ей не дали превратиться
в лохмотья, подновив, наполнили
другим содержанием и заставили
жить. Как заставляют жить
глубоких сирийских старух
новые эмигранты, чтобы было,
кому смотреть за детьми.

Regina Derieva

SECOND-HAND

Buying second-hand clothes
is easy and convenient.
You are not responsible for them,
since they already had an owner,
who did with them what he wanted.
These clothes always go out of fashion.
But here's an article
whose price is a bargain:
having a previous smell,
and a previous mood,
this clothing in essence has died,
but has not turned to tatters,
having been renewed,
having been filled by others,
having been forced to live.
As new emigrants are forced to live,
a very old Syrian woman
looking
after their children.

Translated from the Russian by Frederick Smock

Regina Derieva

Бесполезное занятие

Хороших впечатлений так мало,
что начинаешь их собирать.
Коллекционировать. Бесполезное
занятие. Как если бы
собирать облака. Почему, впрочем,
нет. Это облако я уже
встречала по дороге из Иерусалима
в Вифлеем.
Золото и лазурь прерафаэлитов,
застрявшее на чек-пойнте.

Regina Derieva

Useless Occupation

I do not have enough good impressions
to begin to collect them.
To collect. Useless
occupation. Might as well
collect clouds. However, why not?
This cloud, for example, I just
met on the road from Jerusalem
to Bethlehem.
Gold and azure of the pre-Raphaelites,
it got stuck at the checkpoint.

Translated from the Russian by Frederick Smock

Tony O'Keeffe

The Turn

On the train to Sibiu, Romania

For Andrei Derascu

Stubborn against the cold, these white spring flowers.
Under a grey and pressing sky the land
Slides by, more sea than earth, wind-stirred, wide-green.
What creatures stir—a dog alert for . . . what?
A skimming blackbird, placid morning cows—
Are all the morning offers of warm life.

One bare dead tree, one small bird's silhouette—
The memory of winter in the mind.
Soon the great turn that all this waits upon.
The hours go, carry their deaths, their births.
I watch, within a distance made by glass;
Without, the unfired world, almost.

Maria Tori

Your House, A Room

There are times when you may sit awake
Some hour of the night and realize yourself
Sitting there, alone, with only lamp light
and shadows with you in the room.

It will be so stark and clear that your apartment
Is really just a room in a house.
With four other rooms and four other lives
Occasionally coughing, fucking, and yelling or playing loud music.

The dust will have settled on the surfaces of your things,
Going nowhere just as you are.
Life will seem smaller and more impossible.
Light will fade so that there is just enough for
Darkness to exist.

Chelsie Taylor

Moths in Sage

I bent to pick up
a cigarette butt
and it fluttered away.

It was, after all,
not something discarded,
but a moth
with a flat black head
and dusty-looking wings.

It made me think
of Dad
smoking on the porch
in the almost-dark,
watching the night creatures
land all along
his row of Russian sage.

Andrea Doll

To the White Boy on Bardstown Road

The new orange cream flavor
at the ice cream store
had too much cream
not enough orange

The cicadas on the sidewalk
aren't quite all dead
a dying one flings its panicked body at me
then goes still

I see a thrilled kid
with his head catching the breeze out the window of a car
he's singing the lyrics of song

He looks at me
and when he sees me look back
he smiles
and raises his voice so that I could be an audience
to his performance

A moment passes
and I hear him sing
his final words:

"*Move it*
White Bitch!"

Elsa Cross

Canción

No habría estado jamás bajo tu sombra
si los claveles rojos no se ensañaran
contra la tarde gris.
No habría estado bajo el recuerdo de tu sombra
perfilando en un muro su vuelo detenido.
No habría estado bajo el nombre de tu sombra,
si de su imagen no quedara
esa clara substancia—

Todo se inmoviliza en las ramas
contra el atardecer.
Se ha escondido la luz tras una plancha opaca,
puerta que defiende al corazón
de tu sombra tumultuosa,
de sus canciones lúgubres.

Elsa Cross

Song

I would never have been under your shadow
if the red carnations did not clash
with the gray afternoon.
I would not have been under the memory of your shadow,
outlining on a wall its stopped flight.
I would not have been under the name of your shadow,
if its image had not left
that clear essence—

Everything pauses in the branches
against the sunset.
The light is hidden behind an opaque plate—
a door that defends the heart
from your tumultuous shadow,
from your dismal songs.

Translated from Spanish by Susan Ayres

Sarah Landenwich

Resolution

Today, care for yourself
as if you, too, were a child
who requires laughter as well as sleep,
who wants someone to marvel
at the prize of a fat stick
discovered on the sidewalk
and the sock fuzz caught between her toes.
Someone to notice also
when it is time to put it all away
until tomorrow.
You were that child once.
You were too small to remember
how it felt—
the stick in your hand, the sun
drying the snot on your cheeks to
a glistening film.
Think of this when you reach into
that bottomless need to finish
the emails and dishes, the endless work
of keeping up:
You were her once.
Someone loved you like that.

Greg Pape

Kyoto Hillside

This ancient city laid out by emperor Kanmu
In the eighth century, modeled after
The old capitol of Chang'an in China,
Has survived earthquakes, typhoons, floods,
Fires, famines, plagues, and wars,
With no doubt more to come,
But today from this spot on a hillside
Above Ginkakuji looking down
On the Silver Pavilion and the raked
And calm sea of sand beside the temple
And the main hall where Buson's crows
Go on flying through the hazy summer air,
Low mountains in the distance, one can see
How the houses have lined themselves up
On the hillside but stopped to leave
The hilltop green with trees.
Beside this path rocks lie
Where they have fallen against each other
In a jumble of repose as moss slowly
Thickens and spills its greens
From rock to rock lighting up in a pool
Of sunlight, darkening in shade.
To touch the moss is to feel the green
Changing beneath one's fingers
And the sound of water,
A half inch wide ribbon
Falling six feet through dappled light
And shadow into a small pool,
Enfolds us all and holds this place together.

J. R. Solonche

The Poem of the Future

The poem of the future will be smaller.
It will fit in the palm of your hand,
on your wrist, in your ear.

The poem of the future will not need
bulky batteries or cumbersome wires.
It will be powered by moonlight and weed.

The poem of the future will be automatic.
It will go for months without routine maintenance.
It will be faster, smoother, with a digital tick.

The poem of the future will be lighter.
It will be made of plastics and exotic metals.
It will be available in hundreds of shapes and colors.

The poem of the future will make our lives true.
It will perform in a second what it takes
the poem of the present a day to do.

The poem of the future will talk to us.
It will say things like "Buy IBM," and "Be my friend,"
and "Pulvis et umbra sumus."

J. R. Solonche

La poesia del futuro

La poesia del futuro più piccola sarà.
Nel palmo della mano, sul polso,
nell'orecchio ti starà.

La poesia del futuro non necessiterà
batterie possenti o farragini di fili.
Andrà a erba ed energia lunare.

La poesia del futuro automatica sarà.
Durerà mesi senza manutenzione routinaria.
Sarà più rapida, più fluida, con tick digitale.

La poesia del futuro sarà più lieve.
Sarà fatta di plastica e metalli esotici.
Sarà fruibile in centinaia di forme e di colori.

La poesia del futuro renderà le nostre vite vere.
In un secondo eseguirà quello che prende
alla poesia del presente un giorno intero.

La poesia del futuro ci parlerà.
Cose tipo "Compra IBM" e " Siimi amico" ci dirà,
e "Pulvis et umbra sumus."

Translated to Italian by Angela D'Ambra

Marcia L. Hurlow

Train to Busan

—after Joo-Suk Park

And just before his eyes turn the milky
marble that marks each zombie, he recalls

the birth of his daughter. A blanket
forms a nest. She's a pearl in the center,

unfurling into head and limbs. She stands,
reaches toward him, then opens her star eyes,

first lights from the round haze of her face.
Her gaze is a full life and his judgement.

His struggle ends. He will never see her
again. He cannot take her with him. He

pauses at the back of the train. It crosses
Nakdong River. He enters the current.

Christopher Buckley

Ars Poetica

Lu Ji (261-303)

General, minister, poet,
you never had a chance . . .
A brush at the tip of your mind
touched the eight borders
of the world, all the seas—
you recognized that
there are many styles,
but that the mind
requires precision.

The *Wen Fu*—your treatise
on the art of writing—
was too dazzling
for a jealous court,
and you were undone
by political intrigue
midway in life.
Your last night on earth
was spent wondering
if you would ever again
hear the cranes
of your home
in *Huading*?

There is an ode
for each cloud,
all the heavens to fill
with the unflagging attention
of the heart.
                    A wise man
would give his life
to this instead

of the skills of war,
if he could just let
his ambition drift away. . . .

Every night now,
the shifting stars
remind me
that we are alone
on the earth, no matter
what we say.

John Surowiecki

An Old Man Asleep

Volcanoes spit out teachers.
The sea gives up children, his and maybe his,
getting sick on sundaes and root beer.
Beach roads are crowded with old friends.

One by one they tell him he won't ever die.
No disease will take him, no accident will befall him.
Nothing will end with him,
just one beginning after another

and all that time to think about all that time
and all those times needing to be made right,
life to reassess and loves to leave
exactly as they were.

Jason Tandon

I Finally Tried It

in memory of Mary Oliver

On a hot spring day
when midges spawn and spasm
above the raked plots of dormant grass,
I filled the feeder
with an Eastern songbird blend—
black oil sunflower, cracked corn and millet—
removed my shoes, my socks,
laid down,
wiggled my toes
and waited.

Claudia Buckholts

Immigration

Among reeds flourish cigarette
butts, a cracked snorkel mask,
discarded maps. At the end,
you come here to sit on the wall

watching boats sail out to sea,
dragging their silver nets.
It would be easy to immigrate,
to cross from life's country

into another. The dead possess
this world entire; untethered to
any location, they visit grasslands
where elk labor in silence to graze

and the shoe-top mountain
where wild goats cavort
in the shadows of the moon.
Lights gleam in fog, the cry

of multitudinous souls. You
let your shoulder bag go,
watch it float out to sea.
Your fingers summon winds

that blow from the farthest
corners of the world. You hear
larks calling, song-weaver, who
made your own out of silence,

the deserted beach, the strung
cables that sweep under the sea.

Lynne Potts

As Once a Gift

Time, a flimsy nightgown on the yard's clothesline you try
to hold or write down but it's the wind.

A red lacquered box opens to August in Ukraine with smells
of poplars lining the long road to Odessa on the inside.

Also a flimsy memory that can, strangely, be both dark
and opened like tissue bunched inside that box.

Tissue paper, like other lines written from you to me
who had been there, the poplars, and can still remember.

Then someone asks, *Who made a box that could float the mind from
the living room of a Boston winter to delicate Odessa?*

The answer is moonlit wind that comes and goes in its own whimsical
way; time, the wrinkled tissue dropped to the floor.

As if those presents could be opened again, held up and admired
like the frail lace of that French cotton nightgown

As if there were all the time in the world to write it down
so you would remember me, Grandfather's cuff box

Set on a bureau in his bedroom on Brighton Avenue in Detroit
all the way from Alsace seventy years ago.

Sarah McCartt-Jackson

Borrow

We borrow from the land what we can but cannot
return to it: bluestem, coneflower, boneset, broomcorn,
a ring-necked pheasant tied to a pole, a flat stretch of land
we strip and tar and pave, a creek that gets deeper
as it downrivers, its edges spoiled with runoff.
We collect seeds from the coneflowers and sow them
like quilt pieces, a little scrap of prairie rose here,
scrap of meadowlark feather there. Tamp down
the soil with plodding hooves, steel-toed boots.
Listen as the tallgrass rattles its dry stems,
cottonwood leaves quake as they remember mountain
lakes. Listen to the grain trucks rumble the highway.
We startle at the deer who startle at our footsteps.
A tree frog croaks from its harddark hole in
the otherwise empty change slot of a vending machine.

Nicholas Korn

Wild Sonnet #99

Are we not unto each other bound
As ink and paper are? Each act and utterance
You perform are upon me printed,
As are daily mine on you. Dictation,
Diary and duet at once, a composing paired
Where every moment, line and level look
To be inscripted in each other's book.

Let me recite then what I see and know:
That we are to each—the other's hinted half—
Which hold just out of reach. But for the mirror's
Mention, I do not see the pigment
And parameter my fronted figure paints,
But the illustration of what ill-conceives
The all of yours that's lettered on the leaves.

John James

Poem for My Father Playing a Guitar

Somewhere in the tangled
threadwork of these pages

there's a photo

of my father in a blue
button-up shirt leaning over

the nickel strings

of his guitar. He's just come
home from the chemical plant

where the spiders

make their nests,
& their webs, spun

in factory dark, become

schematics by which to read
the scarlet

hourglasses of their bellies.

My mother & I sing
blindly beside him.

I remember

the wood was black,
& the neck, stained

a deep brown, faded

into silver cross-marks
over which his fingers danced.

Then there are

the days he's lying in bed,
& because we went

skiing in the mountains,

& for weeks after
he was sick, because

in the hospital

he slept for days,
& because we brought him tulips,

I thought he had

pneumonia. Now that
his image is faded

& I recall him only

as a blurred outline
drifting in the midst

of great crowds, I do not

envy him in the least.
All he left behind is

the color of his shirt,

shoes pressed with
the imprint of his feet—

a browning representation

of himself leaning
over a guitar, & a song

I think he's singing,

which I know
I'll never hear.

Olga-Maria Cruz

FROM BRIGHT PANDEMIC MORNING

—poems inspired by the website Window-Swap

Xiaoyou Has a Window

Monday, August 17, 2020

on Chongqing, China,
a long, modern set of three black-framed panes,
cream sheers pulled off to one side.
Their view looks over a mass of trees and greenery,
then into the city, full of other modern high-rises.
A river runs through it, wide and brown, taking
up the left square of glass. Clouds hang unmoving
over the distant buildings. No boats go by.

But Xiaoyou has a telescope, aimed
out the window
toward the city across the river.
So I imagine
that on summer evenings,
you can see the stars.

Olga-Maria Cruz

from Bright Pandemic Morning

—poems inspired by the website Window-Swap

Aoife Has Wandered Far from Home

Saturday, August 8, 2020, 11:32 am

Her name is perfectly Irish but her window
is on the fourth floor of a condo in the UAE,
Al Marjan Island. It's one of those manufactured
pristine islands in the Arabian desert,
perfect carved crescents knifing out
into the Persian Gulf.

I hear Aoife puttering in the kitchen,
without music or chatter.
I wonder if, like me, she likes
to listen to an audiobook
or a podcast while she cooks.

No neighbors on their glass-walled balconies;
just dark rocks below and turquoise water,
completely flat this morning.
An oil rig in the distance.

But now Aoife is sitting down to eat
with me/us/alone. Small adjustments
of the camera as she comes to sit beside it.

I wonder if she feels our presence.

Olga-Maria Cruz

FROM BRIGHT PANDEMIC MORNING

—poems inspired by the website Window-Swap

I'm Curious

Friday, July 31, 2020

about all the other windows.
How many there are, where
I will go next if I click
"*Open a new window*
somewhere in the world"...

Yesterday, heedless as a toddler
and as easily bored,
I clicked through Malaysia (traffic)
and Scotland (river), India (rooftops),
Canada (quirky container garden)
and watched an old woman
hanging up wet clothes in China,
before settling in for the afternoon
on an Amsterdam canal,
the open window framing
five-story buildings, cars, cyclists,
boats on water.

Might not this become its own addiction?
For those of us alone in quarantine,
and those shut in week after week
with the same people. Somehow this escape
is more powerful than games or movies.

I imagine a young child, a someday novelist,
conjuring the lives behind the webcams,
the lives outside the windows. Naming the cats

on the ledges. Researching the species of plants.
Falling asleep to the sound of boats in a harbor
five thousand miles away.

Non-Fiction

Corie Neumayer

About Sunday Morning: A Statement from the Cover Artist

I have always loved to paint landscapes with big loose drippy brush marks and leave splashes and splatters of paint wherever they landed. Exploring a variety of paints and ways to apply them to a canvas has constantly fascinated me. I paint mostly with latex and some standard acrylics on canvas. My colors have always been strong, warm, saturated. I painted fields, hills, and trees in all seasons. Any evidence of people in my work was rare.

Then the Pandemic came. The world kept changing, and I kept changing along with it, and so did my art.

Recovery from surgery, cold grey weather, being quarantined, all made me feel isolated and long for something different. Loose smears of color no longer seemed appropriate. Until I started this series, I had no desire to paint with flat color. Creating form and texture remained a goal. But now all I wanted was clean light bright colors with sharp definite edges, along with some evidence that people existed. It was satisfying to work within these self-imposed limitations, but much more difficult than I ever imagined. It was a world that only looked real to me after much, much repainting.

Sunday Morning expressed my wish for a time when people once again could leave their homes, go out for a stroll, and meet friends at a coffee shop for pastries and conversation. The painting was still a landscape at heart. There was a horizon line with gentle, light ochre hills. Below this, light bright overlapping colors were stacked. A few dark blue lines appeared, possibly representing lingering doubts about the future. The lower half of the painting contained shapes that could be parts of buildings. They directed attention to two rectangles in the center, one a light fresh green, the other the same intense blue as lines at the top. Only a thin, red line separated the dark blue shape from more joyous colors.

Sarah Gorham

"Benedictus," *Requiem*, by Wolfgang Amadeus Mozart

The Rehearsal

I'm one of a dozen invited to attend the final rehearsal of Mozart's *Requiem* in Whitney Hall at the Kentucky Center for the Arts. Unfortunately, when I arrive downtown, I discover that Main Street is under construction with several detours down to the river and back before I can enter the public parking lot, itself a labyrinth stretching below ground an entire block. There are too many elevators, too little information, and my animal fear sets in. I surface at the wrong end of the block, hurry back along an alley, only to discover the Center itself is under construction and all doors are locked. Ah, but here's a clue, three other guests, waving me towards the security entrance, tucked behind an enormous loading dock. And, behind them is the conductor himself, huffing along, one hand on his bicycle. He's dressed in black—jeans, sneakers, Neoprene jacket, helmet, and worn leather backpack. No worries, the rehearsal will not start without him.

We file into a mirrored staging room where a disheveled throng of musicians (chorus and orchestra) is seated on the floor. There are no chairs, only a small table and a piano. Today is the first and only time the two groups will rehearse together before the performances on Friday and Saturday. Yes, they have practiced separately, but in smaller rooms, not even remotely similar to a hall that seats more than twenty-four hundred people. Today, they all crowd through the exit door, amble down a series of corridors, and finally up onto the stage. This is where we part. I choose a spot in the middle of the performance hall, row K, seat twenty-eight.

More than forty years ago, my cousin and I snuck into one of the Kennedy Center Opera House's faux velvet box seats to witness our first performance of Mozart's majestic, heart-rending *Requiem Mass*. We were there late, but as each section unfolded—the Sequentia, Offertorium, Sanctus, Benedictus, Agnus Dei, and Communio—we turned to each other in giddy astonishment. What serendipity, what an extraordinary gift. It was so much worth the risk of being caught without a ticket. Afterwards, we both headed to a record store and purchased the Neville Mariner 1977 recording on vinyl, which was eventually replaced by cassette tape, CD, and MP3, etc. And now, decades later, the chance of hearing it live again, just a few miles from my home in Louisville, was almost too good to be true.

The stage crew has neglected to set up risers for the chorus, or even chairs, so they're forced to stand through the entire rehearsal or, when idle, sit on the floor. From my seat, the first row of singers drops out of sight, obscured by four soloists in front, and the strings, percussion, woodwinds, and brass in-between. This will be corrected of course, but for now it makes the conductor's job a little more difficult. The chorus will have to project over both orchestra and soloists with clarity of diction, volume, texture, and phrasing, so that an audience will understand it, all at his direction. It's not an unusual challenge. One of the reasons there's a conductor in the first place is that the brass can't necessarily hear what the strings are playing, and the last stand violins are on the opposite side of the stage from the basses. What the cellos are playing may not carry, particularly above the brass. Our conductor complains that he can't hear the soloists either. For now, he asks them to rotate towards him, but while they are waiting for their cues, they slip back little by little and turn towards the house. I'm not disappointed for I love to watch them close-up. Even when silent, it's obvious the music is working inside them. With her forehead, the soprano nudges the air rhythmically, taps her sensible shoe along with the opening movements. With forefinger and thumb, the tenor wobbles his windpipe. The bearded bass might fit in well at a hipster coffee shop until he begins to sing. And what a sound he makes.

Is it all mush? The conductor asks, throwing his question into the cavernous space we're scattered in. Not to my uneducated ears. I give the thumbs up.

Today, with so many musicians on hand, not to mention union requirements and restrictions, the conductor doesn't have the luxury of micro-managing—stopping, re-starting, and polishing each measure or phrase. Five minutes of overtime might cost $750 or more. He must set priorities and make sure the rehearsal touches upon each one. High on the list is familiarizing the chorus with the *Requiem*'s pacing, tempo and, I repeat, the venue itself. That's something that not many people realize—you can't move musicians from a university practice room to an enormous hall without adjustments. The acoustics are not the same, thus equalizing is one of a conductor's most important tasks, making him more of a sound producer, as if he were seated in front of a large computer, adjusting, and balancing the volume for the bass, guitar, and drums, as well as the vocals and backups—responsible for making sure the audience can hear everything, even when vocals or drums or the bass might dominate at certain points. Essentially, he's live mixing, as if stationed before a console of knobs, buttons and faders in a recording studio. Imagine doing this with a hundred plus performers, in one rehearsal, all within a two-and-a-half-hour time frame, including a fifteen-minute break. And today, after the break, they'll run-through the other feature of the night—selections from Monteverdi's *Vespers to the Virgin Mary*, a monstrously difficult piece.

Surreptitiously I glance at my watch, not because I'm bored. Far from it. I'm afraid they'll take a break and move onto the Monteverdi before we ever hear the Benedictus, my priority, the reason I'm here today.

"By the way," the conductor says as the last notes die out, "That was great," and the musicians stamp their feet.

The Benedictus

The Benedictus is a breath of fresh air and a glorious, mellifluent break from the sorrow and angst of the funeral mass. It falls close to the end, after the Sanctus. Its "barbershop quartet" is the primary feature, cast in B♭ major, a key described by one of Mozart's contemporaries, the German poet and organist Christian Schubart, as "a quaint creature often dressed in the garment of night," her sound characterized by "cheerful love, clear conscience, and aspiration for a better world."

Indeed, these are the thoughts that come to mind as the "A" theme is introduced by the alto, followed after just two measures by the soprano and, in due course, the tenor and bass, weaving in and out, like a square dance allemande left, only far more sophisticated and elaborate. The four voices resolve on a held Benedictus, and what else could we be thinking of at this point but world peace and love? And what other musical phrase could follow this note than the Hosanna, a fugue picked up from the Sanctus, also in the bright key of B♭ major?

There are only six words in the lyric: *Benedictus qui venit in nomine Domini*, or "Blessed is He who comes in the name of the Lord." Unlike much of the *Requiem*, they are full of hope and the sweet reassurance that Jesus, Son of God, has finally arrived to take away the sins of the world. Even if you do not believe, it's difficult to resist this miraculous sound traveling from beyond our knowing, landing as it did in the brain of one particular genius—Johannes Chrysostomus Wolfgangus Theophilus Mozart, who "carried the message" to us. No wonder Tchaikovsky referred to him as "the musical Christ."

Mozart *was* a divine master of melody, even as a child. According to family accounts, his compositions often began with a simple improvisation, composed in his head or on the piano. Then, under conscious control, he heaped on complicated variations and transformations. There might be three or four melodies going at once, each of them self-contained and complete. I never grow tired of his overlapping lines that have been floating unbidden through my consciousness for decades. Mozart was a master of equilibrium, that sought-after state of mind so beautifully realized here—in texture (monophonic, polyphonic) tempo (andante and allegro), dynamics (crescendo, decrescendo), color through orchestration (woodwinds and strings), and of course, harmony. In the Benedictus, lyricism—song, expression, even poetry—is really on show. And blessedly, the soloists are granted phrases they can execute in a single breath. The singers dip and sway, eyebrows raise, lids close and open. It feels natural to mirror them with my body, and the temptation to sing along is irresistible.

Much later, alone in my house, I return to this movement, raise the volume, and mimic Teddy's movements. I'm not *actually* conducting, that would be ridiculous. But I'm not satisfied with sedentary listening. No, my body aches to fully participate, so I let go a little—rock on my feet, lift my arms ever-so-slightly, extend my thumbs and fingers to their tips, where I signal to the winds, the violins, the timpani, then the soprano, alto, tenor, bass, then all four voices in unison. What else can I do? The *Requiem* in its entirety is music *wrestling with death.* But for me, the Benedictus is transcendence itself: *Qui venit in nominee Domini Osanna in excelsis!*

Then I remember with a tinge of dismay that the Benedictus, as well as the Sanctus, Agnus Dei, and Communio, were largely the work of Franz Xavier Süssmayr, though the authorship of these sections is still under discussion. To subsist, Mozart relied heavily on assignments from the court; he wrote for money, not posterity. After his death, his wife Constanze was in financial distress, in dire need of the final installment of Count Franz Walsegg-Stuppach's commission (which, incidentally, he planned to pass off as his own). Süssmayr was Mozart's copyist and assistant, a friend of the family, and a logical choice for the task. He was also a great admirer, familiar with the compositions, and careful to attend to Mozart's vision. Constanze naturally turned to him to complete the *Requiem*. He managed to finish the job in just a hundred days, this from a few pages of disorganized sketches found on the composer's desk, and Mozart himself, who had conveyed instructions from his deathbed. Süssmayr also borrowed heavily from completed material, including the Introit. One could accurately describe his additions as imitative.

Only a portion of Mozart's original score for the *Requiem* survives today. Quite extraordinary that anything survived, when you consider the fragility of paper and its necessarily spare usage in the eighteenth century. Parchment was very expensive; composers had to avoid mistakes and cram as much music on the page as they could, thus the compressed appearance of staves, which were drawn by hand with a five-quill pen. So much disappeared along with Mozart's death—lost or thrown away by his widow. One remaining page was stolen from an exhibition at the 1958 World's Fair in Brussels. A corner is torn off that might contain the last words Mozart ever wrote: "Quam olim," his note from the Introit to suggest the *Domine Jesu* fugue should be repeated. The ragged morsel of paper has never been found.

There have been arguments about Süssmayr's contributions for over two hundred years. More than sixty years ago, the German publisher Bärenreiter-Verlag launched the massive scholarly publication of all of Mozart's works, *Die Neue Mozart-Ausgabe*. Today, it contains a hundred and thirty-two volumes, with twenty-five thousand pages of music, as well as critical commentaries, forewords, and numerous supplements. It is considered the definitive edition for scholars, composers, and musicians, based on all available authentic sources, though primarily on Mozart's scores and sketches. In its entry for the *Requiem*, there's a particular emphasis on identifying precisely who wrote what parts of the Mass. Attributions are indicated by an "M" or "S" at the beginning of each section and it's clear the "S" dominates the further in you go.

Many critics claim that where the music is strongest, it must be

Mozart's. The errors or weak points are attributed to his assistant. And the quality of Süssmayr's work continues to be debated: the Sanctus, for example, has been simultaneously described as "superb" by some, and "one of the worst sections" of the Mass by others.

I wonder how much I should take this to heart. Imagine buying what you thought was an original Rembrandt that, after consultation, turned out to be an apprentice's work worth half the price? Rembrandt used studio assistants to complete his portraits. Does that make the paintings less great? Similarly, the most expensive violins might have a Stradivarius body with refurbished parts, or a neck fashioned by another luthier, but if the violins create that sought-after sound, why the concern?

Instead, the *Requiem* could be imagined as a kind of musical pentimento. Mozart's figures and drafts shone through Sussmayer's contributions and there were earlier composers who formed another layer beneath Mozart's own creations. He had a prodigious memory and a gift for mimicking the music he heard around him. He looked backwards as he wrote, infusing his compositions with elements of Bach and Handel and earlier composers, sometimes borrowing in full. Some scholars, for example, like to point out similarities in the Introitus and Kyrie to *Messiah*'s "He Hath Borne Our Griefs," followed by "And with His Stripes." As the saying goes: if you must steal, steal from the greats. Mozart, it seems, might have anticipated the pastiche and collage of post-modernism well before modernism even occurred.

If the music is important, beautiful, and widely beloved, does it really matter if it's made of something old and something new, a little borrowed or blue?

The Conductor

In 2014, the conductor Teddy Abrams traveled from Brooklyn to our fair city to lead the Louisville Orchestra, which had struggled with dwindling audiences and budget shortfalls for a number of years. He arrived with a superlative dossier, including orchestra stints in Budapest, Washington, Houston, Phoenix, Jacksonville, San Francisco, Vancouver, Indianapolis, Florida, and Detroit; as well as the Colorado, North Carolina, New Jersey, New World Symphonies; and the Louisiana and New Mexico Philharmonics. He studied with Michael Tilson Thomas, Otto-Werner Mueller, and Ford Lallerstedt at the Curtis Institute, the youngest student ever accepted there. Some of his event tickets sell in the four digits. Others are free. He is a concert-level soloist on piano and clarinet. He has jammed with My Morning Jacket and curated an entire stage at the wildly popular festival Forecastle, closing it with his band Teddy Abrams & Friends. When he took up his position in Louisville as Conductor and Musical Director, he was just twenty-seven.

I've watched a conductor's gestures and seen chop, pierce, and sever. I've also imagined a baker—mixing, whipping, and folding. Others have compared these motions to the crest, trough, and face of a wave. In any case, gesture is the thing when communicating artistic directions—with baton, forefinger, pinky or thumb, both arms and whole body. The right hand traces a fully formed figure for every measure. The upbeat comes first, a stroke skyward. It reveals nothing in itself, just a fleeting promise, as when praying for luck we generally point our fingers to the heavens like miniature steeples—what's to come may be cheerful or grave.

The downbeat comes second. A mere flick of the wrist for the precise moment when it lands on the *ictus*, Latin for "blow." In an extended solo, a conductor may keep up the rhythm with a tap on the music stand (a continuous flow of beats called *takt*—German for bar, measure, and beat) and cue the musicians by establishing eye contact, or merely sniff in their direction. Larger motions indicate an increase in volume, leaning back for a hush. These are just some of the ways a conductor influences a performance, and every conductor too has his or her own idiosyncratic gestural language.

In his Market Street apartment, Teddy spent over eighteen months studying, analyzing, experimenting, researching, and reading every bar of the *Requiem* till he found a way through to an interpretation that was both historical and unique. To lead, he has to be thoroughly familiar with the piece, on top of it before the music even happens. The Benedictus opens with a phrase from the basset horns, Mozart's favorites with their darker pitch and reedier feel, mostly substituted in our time by clarinets. Other instruments will repeat this phrase later in variation. But it's likely that each group of instrumentalists is too focused on its own contributions to be aware of this pattern. The conductor must be conscious of both—the serial words and the full narrative. I can visualize Teddy at the piano, leafing through his score as if he were reading a novel.

I played the piano for eight years, beginning at age seven, occasionally performing for a small group of parents and students in Mrs. Jacobson's backyard studio. What I remember clearly are the Sara Lee brownies and Hawaiian Punch in paper cups laid out on her polished coffee table. Less fondly, the anxiety and constant practicing at our family's enormous upright. It took many days to master a short Sarabande from Bach's *French Suites*—the correct notes and fingering, then the phrasing, accents, and slurs. Once I had it down, I added color and feeling. I was particularly concerned about that feeling. Our living room was separated from the dining room by a pair of pocket doors; I wanted to be sure they were ajar and all four of my sisters were sufficiently moved as my performance steadily improved.

At the very least, no one complained. But after Mrs. Jacobson passed away, another teacher took over, and wanted to hear the Sarabande for herself. After only a minute, she grabbed my right arm and said, "Oh, I'm sorry. That is *way* too schmaltzy."

In the Japanese art of bonsai, the instructions are clear: the maker's touch should be invisible. If wiring is necessary, it must be concealed or eventually removed entirely. When a branch is clipped, there cannot be any visible scars or lasting impressions on the bark. This aesthetic ensures that the message of *wabi sabi* comes through unimpeded: nothing lasts, nothing is finished, and nothing is perfect.

In one of his more grouchy moods, Stravinsky preached something similar: "We do not wish any so-called interpretations of our music, just play the notes, add nothing, and take nothing away." The composer was responding to a scourge of exaggerating and falsifying interpreters, the prima donnas of his time. It was one thing to shape the music. These folks had gone too far, injecting their personalities to an outlandish degree, even to the point of changing the notes. He advised that they allow the music to speak for itself. In other words—restrain your ego and "just play the ink."

Stravinsky put down plenty of ink. Accents, staccatos with an accent on top, tenutos with an accent, tenutos with a staccato, sometimes perhaps fifteen different articulations on top of these little notes. At certain points the editors of *Die Neue Mozart-Ausgabe* added asterisks, forcing a player to glance down at the bottom of the pages, where there might be several unique shades of dynamics. Triple piano, mezzo piano "but not too much." Elongated tempos, *getragen, hält*—from the German meaning "stately" and "held onto."

Better to approach a piece of music as a "living organism," adding the slightest bit of personality, but mostly attending to the style of the period in which the music was written. Or perhaps "musicality" is a more accurate term—what the truly great performers have in spades—talent, technique, knowledge, sensitivity, and a pure integration of all these elements. All in the name of carrying the full story to their audiences.

Mozart wasn't much for ink. His earliest sketches were just bits and pieces on a page, with most of the music swimming in his head. Later he added the melody and perhaps a bass line. He then laid these scores aside as "finished compositions." Still later, he filled in the harmonies and many of the remaining notes. These, he called "written." If you look closely at the original score to the Benedictus, the basics are there, but not much else. Great swatches move along with little to suggest character. Articulations are sparse: I could find mostly *tenuto,* only a snippet of *staccato,* and no accents at all—this across all staves. The dynamics too—*mezzoforte, piano, fortissimo,* and crescendo—are scattered parsimoniously through the music.

The Pathos

> *"For one moment in the history of music all opposites were reconciled; all tensions resolved; that luminous moment was Mozart."*
> —Phil G. Goulding

Let's go back to the idea of a wave, which, in music, can be tied to more than the upswing and plunge of a baton. A wave has a crest and a trough, peaks and withdrawals, the wind in between stirring, nudging, heaving the water to its short-lived apogee. Then it crashes and the action begins all over again. It's a cycle we see across all life, whether it's ocean, planet, or human existence. Indeed, the smallest pieces of matter—particles—also behave as waves. Musicians make use of this pattern, this rhythm of erosion and lift, majors and minors, crises, and resolutions.

The *Requiem* is cast in D minor, a key Christian Schubert characterized as "discontent, uneasiness, and gnashing of teeth." Through most of Mozart's short life, he focused on the major keys, but as he matured, he inched into C, G, and D minor as well. He wanted his Mass to evoke passion, religious devotion, tragedy, and beauty, elements we might expect to suit the occasion of a funeral.

Every composer makes use of both major and minor—within

chords, phrases, and whole sections—volleying from one key to the other. The *Requiem*'s overall signature of D minor is not the only reason the music is sorrowful. Intervals—the distance between any two notes—play a far more important role. When played successively or simultaneously, the resulting sound can be a consonance, like the perfect fifth or a full octave. If the notes abut like the opening of "Chopsticks," the sound is harsh and disturbing. As Mozart said, "Dissonance is a way by which emotion is expressed." He used it for special effect, following up with bold and complex harmonies, creating a sense of direction and shape. Tension leads to repose and stability, as well as a belief in the harmonious qualities of morality and the goodness of Nature.

Pulling out his phone, Teddy searches for the sheet music with an amazing tool—IMSLP, the International Music Score Library Project—where you can download, many, many pieces of music for free. He swipes through the pages with his thumb till he lands on what he's looking for, then hums along with the notes. "See?" he says. "You can tell where the soloists are repeating the exact same intervals as the violins did earlier. It's a really complex process." He points to a few more of the descending intervals, singing again and "conducting" with his right forefinger. One passage symbolizes the pain and suffering of Jesus on the cross. Teddy describes it as a "downward pull, a little stab that compels you towards an answer."

Pebbles, shells, bits of seaweed and sand are tossed into frenzy until the wave relaxes. Waves of anxiety are followed by reassurance This movement from conflict to relief and back again is a classic gesture, a basic currency that occurs in all music, across art forms, cultures, and nations. Think of that floating place you call sleep and the morning that shatters it. Or a dream that chases you like a bear till someone nudges your shoulder and you're safe. The forbidding shock of death alternating with a merciful, sublime consolation: we hear this a lot in the *Requiem*.

In a highly idealized etching "*Ein Moment aus den letzten Tagen Mozarts*," by Franz Schramm, it's clear the artist has nothing but respect and admiration for the composer. Süssmayr is at his side, poised to take in his instructions. Constanze is bent over a prayer bench in the corner, and a bright "holy" light accents Mozart's formal clothing, the chair he sits in, and the score lying on his lap. By the door, a messenger is just departing, perhaps with news of the imminent death, though the composer appears rather healthy.

Mozart died the fifth of December in 1791 at his home in Vienna. Of the exact details, there are accountings and re-accountings, versions and revisions. He traveled to Prague to oversee the production of his opera *La clemenza di Tito* and fell sick. There was fever, rash, back pain, and considerable swelling. When he returned to Vienna, he gradually slid into his grave.

Or he died suddenly.

He was poisoned, hence the complaints of a metallic taste in his mouth. Later ruled out.

He was afflicted with renal disease, trichinosis, or syphilis.

The treatments themselves—bloodletting and mercury salts—caused Mozart's death.

The most recent research points to a strep infection, a leading cause of death at the time and widespread in Vienna. While Mozart was dying, his eldest son Karl stood by his bedside. Karl later wrote, in a surprisingly clinical manner, "Particularly remarkable is in my opinion the fact that a few days before he died, his whole body became so swollen that the patient was unable to make the smallest movement. Moreover, there was stench, which reflected an internal disintegration which, after death, increased to the extent that an autopsy was impossible," (from Maynard Solomon's *Mozart: A Life*).

In the end, he was buried in a "pauper's grave."

No, it was merely a "common grave," a tradition at the time for anyone who wasn't aristocracy.

The weather was horrible—thunder, lightning, buckets of rain. The weather was mild, with a slight mist.

Mozart composed up until the very end. He often wondered aloud if the *Requiem* was intended for him.

The Concert

Whitney Hall is full to the brim, awash with murmurs and the rustling of programs, coats removed, purses stashed. The applause begins as Teddy Abrams enters stage left. But . . . what's this? He stops short of the podium for a moment of reflection. The news is bad. Twelve worshippers were murdered at a synagogue in Pittsburgh. And just yesterday, a gunman killed four people after a racially motivated rampage at a local Kroger. He asks for a moment of silence and the audience complies. "I don't know about you," he says, "but after a terrible tragedy, I turn to art, especially music, for its ability to draw us together," then pivots slightly, "and so I've asked our mayor to say a few words." The official enters on cue—also from stage left—accepts the microphone, and opens with a joke, "Rest easy, I'm not here to conduct." Then the platitudes roll out for what seems like an eternity: "Refuse to become numb…this is an opportunity for us to be as one . . . let's celebrate our common humanity . . ." etc. He is an excellent mayor, but not much of a priest.

Finally, the conductor steps up and the Introitus sneaks in like a herd of deer on grass. Teddy is all business—flicking his wrists with high precision, extending all ten of his fingers to signal a close, elbows forward and back in rapid succession. Meanwhile, the choir members flip their sheet music. From my seat (this time purchased), way up in Row L, third balcony, the pages might be hundreds of crane wings. The baton leads, tracing whitecaps across the air.

For an annoying five minutes, my concentration is broken by a man seated next to me, slurping his bourbon from a clear plastic cup. Try listening with your eyes closed, my husband says. Okay, I think, but only for a few seconds. Inside, I see a featureless umber screen. No sparkling chandelier and elegant velvet curtains. No enormous kettledrum or piano crowded into a rear stage corner. No Teddy. I could be in my office with headphones on. Why am I here if not to watch the bows slide across the bellies of violins, violas, and cellos? Why refuse the gold snap and flash of trombones, tubas, and other brass? And the musicians dressed in black, perched on the edges of their chairs, their posture impeccable, bolt upright, feet forward? I can't wait till they launch into the Benedictus.

When they do—when the conductor nods, the soloists stand, and the alto leads with the full phrase *Benedictus qui venit in nomine Domini.* The soprano jumps in on the *Domini,* and the bass and tenor enter one after the other on the repeat of Benedictus—and the urge to sing is again overwhelming. I want to participate, to join in with my lips and my tongue and my throat and my lungs and my ribs expanding and contracting. It's the effect of great art, even on non-practitioners. We intuit excellence and intensity and desperately want to do it ourselves. Hence my lifelong obsession to chime in, whether it's with piano, or voice lessons, or especially this essay, which allows me to come the slightest bit closer using my given art form.

I'm deeply familiar with the *Requiem*, and especially the Benedictus. Still, what I hear is so limited—the content precisely in proportion to my scant knowledge, my biases, and inadequate attention span. The music is so large, so God given. How to take it in entirely, every single note, chord, phrase, gesture? If I followed my impulse and broke into song, my neighbor in front would not be pleased. So, I restrain myself, tap discretely with right forefinger on one knee and a barely noticeable tick-tock of my head. Somehow, it's enough: the luxury of the music pouring in, and the *dolce dolore* it carves in my chest once it is over.

Jonathan Weinert

I Couldn't Say No

It was always hard to explain about my mother. If you had met her briefly you might have thought, "What a delightful lady! How nice!" I heard statements like this from any number of distant relations and casual family friends over the years when I was growing up in the 1960s and the 1970s, and it always unsettled me. "You're so lucky to have a mother like that!" they would say, not knowing what she was like when they weren't around.

Mom could be charming and she certainly wasn't stupid, and guests to our house, in our charming suburb west of Boston, always put her on her best behavior. Mom would nod and listen politely and laugh little self-deprecating laughs as she shared some bit of conventional wisdom that she wouldn't have dreamed of applying to herself. Her eyebrows would go up and stay there, and a little cherub's smile would appear, affixed to the lower half of her face. She was pink and round as a dumpling and had a cap of light brown curls on her head, like Shirley Temple in Wee Willie Winkie. She would sit there mildly, hardly moving, the very picture of consideration, while Cousin So-and-So went on about her son's latest stroke of fortune, or Mrs. Thingy held forth on the rumpus that was last month's school committee meeting.

But the moment the friend or relation would leave, the mask would fall, and the bitter, unfriendly face that was hidden behind it would surface. The corners of Mom's mouth would turn down in a thin tight frown, and her bloodless lips would crowd together with the rest of her features in the center of her small dry face.

It was like in the movies. The detectives are making the rounds, and they knock on the door of the villain. We know she has a half a dozen neighborhood kids chained to the plumbing in a crawlspace beneath a hidden trap door, but the cops won't figure it out until later. She invites them in, she clucks sympathetically, she's amiable and a little dotty but apparently harmless; she offers them coffee and apologizes that she has no cookies or cake to go along with it, she laughs a little self-effacing laugh and the cops leave, sorry to have bothered you ma'am, if you hear anything etcetera, but as soon as she closes the front door behind them she turns, all grim determination, and goes back to flaying the skin off her victims.

I witnessed these performances of my mother's with a mixture of bewilderment and hope. They demonstrated, among other things, that she was capable of manipulating the levers of social convention when she wanted to, and that she was able to listen to someone else's story without instantly replacing it with one of her own, as was her habit. Apparently, she actually possessed the capacity to put herself in someone else's shoes—or at least to make a decent imitation of it.

But such proofs put me in a quandary, because Mom never treated me with such consideration. Maybe, my thinking went, if I was good enough and obedient enough and wanted it enough, she might listen to me too. But because it never happened, and because I was a kid and couldn't help it, I blamed myself. If Mom constantly criticized me and found fault with whatever I said and liked and did, I must have deserved it. I was bad, therefore Mom was mean.

Not that I could have confided such misgivings about myself to Mom in any case. Her idea of commiseration was to rehearse her own woes, real or imagined. She habitually complained of being "busy-busy," of being tired ("tie-id," in her Boston accent), that the circumstances of her life were overwhelming.

"Hi Mom, what's going on?" I would say, entering the kitchen as she was preparing the evening's meal of Hamburger Helper and spinach boiled to within an inch of its life.

"Oy! It's been *wild!*" she would reply, not looking up from the stove.

"*What's* been wild?" I would ask, genuinely wanting to know.

"I don't know. I mean, I've been *busy-busy.*"

"Like, doing what?"

"Oh, *you* know. It's like I can hardly *breathe* around here."

But I didn't know, and I was left to guess at the sources of her vexations.

Such exchanges were usually innocuous, but sometimes they turned malignant. Gauging Mom's emotional weather was no idle task. Even when she was ignoring me, her base level of chronic irritation could easily spike, and I never knew what might set her off. The trigger could be anything, or it could be nothing. It was often something trivial, so I had constantly to be on guard.

Mom's abrasiveness and irritation were overt and frequently on display, but her malice was covert and underhanded: you could never exactly put your finger on it. She never swore, and when she stooped to name-calling, as she sometimes did, she enlisted her smattering of Yiddish, as if to veil the insult. She preferred *momzer*, for example, to the blunter and more Latinate *bastard*. She would call me a *pisher* (a contemptible person, a bed-wetter) or a *khazer* (a pig), depending on what supposed failing of mine she wanted to highlight.

Alongside the Yiddish, Mom employed a series of stock phrases and stylized asides, each carrying its own payload of judgment and disdain.

"You're wearing *that shirt*?" Mom would demand, no matter what I was wearing.

"Bully for *you*," she would mutter when I was excited about something.

"Another party is heard from," she would say sarcastically, if I expressed a contradictory opinion.

"The kitchen is *closed!*" she would snap, if I tried to help myself to an after-dinner snack. (Meanwhile, she sat at the kitchen table reading junk mail, her left arm up to the elbow in a bag of Doritos.)

"You're *aroysgevorfen!*" she would exclaim when she was particularly frustrated. This literally meant that I was "thrown away," an article of trash.

The effect of these remarks was cumulative, like water torture. Each incident was merely a drip, but exposure to an endless series of such drips eventually drove me around the bend.

Another kid might have been oblivious enough, or shameless enough, to shrug such treatment off. Not me: I took everything to heart. This was both a strength in me and the source of much pain. It's easier, I suppose, to find fault with others, and excuse yourself for any hint of malfeasance; it may even be a psychologically sound defensive tactic. But I lacked the ability entirely. Everything went into me and stayed there. I was, as they say, *sensitive*. There was something narcissistic about this, of course—ascribing to myself the causes of all my experience. Nevertheless, the message Mom kept sending me had been received, and I believed it: there was something fundamentally wrong with me. I didn't have the strength, or the perspective, to see that it was all projection, a fiction that Mom was intent on perpetuating, because the alternative was inadmissible—for *her*.

One late summer morning in 1969, when I was ten, I was rummaging around in the walk-in closet in the bathroom off the den, looking for a baseball glove. This was a large, echoey, institutional sort of restroom with two windows set high in the wall and an ancient clawfoot bathtub that we never used. Into the closet my parents had pitched an assortment of folding chairs, cast-off hats and unloved jackets, lengths of two-by-four, and leftover tiles from failed renovation projects.

My hand strayed over something unexpected in the dimness, and I pulled it out: an old oil painting jammed way in back behind some sheets of particle board. It was a standard nautical still life featuring colored glass spheres in a fishing net and a stick of driftwood on a table—apparently some sort of student exercise. Mom's name appeared as a bold scrawl in the lower right corner.

"Mom, is this your painting?" I called out, my voice reverberating off the bathroom walls.

I knew it was hers, but discovering it was as odd as finding a diamond in a box of salt, and I wanted to hear her confirm it.

"*Hon*estly!" Mom shouted from the kitchen, where she had started making lunch. "What are you doing schmying around in *that closet*?!"

"Just looking at stuff," I said, resting the painting on the kitchen table. "When did you paint this?"

"I don't know. *High school*."

"Is this your only one?"

"I was gonna be a *painter*. Then I married your *father*."

"So?" I ventured, not quite sure where Mom was going with this.

"So *buttons*."

"Okay, so then you stopped painting? How come?"

"*Please*," Mom said. "I'll write you a *letter*."

As usual, mom's belligerent tone made short work of my desire to ask more questions. I had somehow put my foot wrong, so I returned the painting to the closet and got out of Mom's way.

Soon after this exchange, another piece of artwork in the house touched off another, equally mysterious conversation.

"Mom, who's John Bernhardt, and why do we have his picture up in the kitchen?"

A framed woodcut—a stylized rendering of Monhegan Island, off the coast of Maine—hung on the kitchen wall, opposite the stove. I must have asked about this picture several times over the years, and every time Mom told the story it sounded unfamiliar and new, as if she were making it up as she went along. Like many of Mom's stories, I couldn't remember the details after the fact: they tended to evaporate, like narrative smoke. Follow-up questions didn't occur to me, sometimes, until years later.

A self-satisfied smirk stole across Mom's face. She inclined her head a little downward and to the left, planted her right heel on the floor and flexed her right foot up to signal a sort of casual confidentiality. But there was nothing casual or confiding about Mom.

"I knew John Bernhardt at *Columbia.* Of course, you know Bunny lives in *California*," Mom said, not answering my question. Mom loaded the word "California" with grievance, as if she had something against the Golden State, or maybe against this person named Bunny.

I gave Mom a blank look.

"You know, *Bunny Bernhardt.*"

Oh. So *that* explained it.

"Bunny lives in *Santa Barbara.* I guess she has some life out there. I mean, *psssh*!"

Psssh was a variation on "Wow!", half amazed and half dismissive, and it was invariably accompanied by two twists of Mom's right wrist, her fingers balled into a fist.

"It must be *nice*, living in a place like *Santa Barbara*, with that *weather.* Who knows, someday I might just up and *visit* her there. Try and stop me! Someday when I'm not so *busy-busy*!"

(Wrist, wrist.)

It was clear that Mom had no intention of visiting Bunny in California. I pictured a middle-aged woman reclining by a pool wearing a one-piece bathing suit, dark sunglasses with rhinestone-encrusted frames, and a big floppy sun hat, holding an iced drink in a red-nailed hand.

"When I was at *Columbia*, I worked with *Bertram Wolfe*. Of course, he was a big *Communist,* but what can you do? *Psssh*!"

(Wrist, wrist.)

"He helped me get a job at the *Voice of America*. I mean, this was the *Cold War*. I took classes with *Merle Fainsod* at *Radcliffe*. I mean . . . Your father only got into *Harvard* because of the GI Bill. That's where my Russian came in handy, at the Voice of America."

Mom had majored in German and minored in Russian at Radcliffe.

"Not that I ever *used* the Russian but, you know, it *helped*. Bertram Wolfe actually *thanks* me in the introduction to his *book*."

(Wrist, wrist.)

"It's about *Stalin* and *Lenin*, those types—I mean, not exactly the nicest people—but anyway. I was *there*!"

Mom delivered this last sentence as if I was not going to believe her. I *did* believe her, but weren't we supposed to be talking about John Bernhardt?

This was typical. If you tried to talk to Mom about most anything, she would turn the conversation into a monologue about herself. There were no details about John Bernhardt forthcoming because Mom wasn't really interested in John Bernhardt. John Bernhardt was only a pretext for Mom to enlarge upon her own supposedly extraordinary experiences.

And so I learned nothing about John Bernhardt, well-respected minor abstractionist printmaker, born Indianapolis 1921, married Bunny Pritchard 1948, died suddenly Santa Barbara 1963, of complications from tuberculosis. But how the Bernhardts and my parents met, and how they got to know each other, and whether the friendship had anything to do with Mom's foiled ambitions as an artist, I was never to discover.

You can't really understand a Jewish family without considering guilt. Every Jewish household has its store, to go along with the Shabbos candles and the Seder plate, and ours was no exception.

Guilt is the flipside of responsibility, and the Jews are nothing if not responsible. As God's "Chosen People," the Jews have both assumed responsibility and been held responsible. Because nobody's perfect, guilt shadows every effort to do right, no matter how valiant: there's always something to criticize.

For a long time, I thought Mom was a special case. She laid on the criticisms and personal attacks daily but never once seemed mortified or ashamed, never once apologized. She seemed to feel guilty about precisely nothing. Years later, I realized that exactly the opposite was true. Mom didn't lack guilt; on the contrary, she found her own sense of guilt so overwhelming and intolerable that she had to get rid of it by projecting it onto someone else.

That someone else often turned out to be me. As a scapegoat, I was an inspired choice. I felt guilty about pretty much everything pretty much all of the time, although I couldn't have said why. Even when I lashed out at Mom's relentless insinuations; even when I yelled and screamed at her to leave me alone; even when I felt justified, because somewhere inside me I knew that what Mom was saying was false and what she was doing was wrong: even then, I felt guilty.

Eventually my sense of guilt became so pervasive that it grew to existential proportions—that is to say, I came to feel guilty for merely existing. Of course, this impression didn't come from nowhere: it was strongly, if implicitly, suggested.

Then it was explicitly suggested.

A humid midsummer weeknight, 1973. My younger brother, who was only seven, was already asleep. Dad was reading the day's *Globe* in the big living room chair with his feet up on a hassock, or holding the paper up and pretending to read. Mom was in the dining room, translating articles on Russian aviation for the Air Force, recent issues of *Pravda* and other Soviet broadsheets piled everywhere.

As a fourteen-year-old, I was too young to have started smoking weed, and I was never really interested in drinking. Reality, on the other hand, was often too much for me to take, so I determined to get drunk and see what it might do for me.

My parents weren't big drinkers, to say the least, so there were always open bottles of liquor in the cabinet above the kitchen stove. I listened at my bedroom door to make sure that the coast was clear, then sneaked downstairs. I opened the liquor cabinet doors as quietly as possible, selected a half-finished bottle of cheap Smirnoff vodka that had been sitting in there for god knows how long, grabbed an orange plastic cup from the dish drain, and poured myself a large measure.

I replaced the vodka bottle, silently closed the cabinet doors, tiptoed back up to my room cup in hand, and chugged. The vodka tasted awful and it burned, but I choked it down—all of it, in one huge wallop. Then I looked around, uncertain as to what would happen next. I rinsed out the plastic cup in the upstairs bathroom and made my way back downstairs as the alcohol started taking effect. Suddenly, I found myself overwhelmed by an invasion of affectionate feeling. I didn't know where it came from, but I felt filled up to the brim with love—filled up and spilling over.

Mom had moved to the kitchen table, where she was reading the previous Sunday's *Parade* magazine. For a second, I thought that she had discovered my raid on the liquor cabinet and was giving me the silent treatment, but she seemed oblivious and didn't look up.

A flood of compassion washed over me. I felt a fierce and deeply rooted love for this woman who often behaved so unkindly toward me. I stood in the kitchen doorway and tried to take her in—really take her in and *see* her. If only I could say the right words, maybe I could break through the hard feelings. Maybe we could make a real connection, Mom and I, and express our true feelings to one another, even if it was only for a moment.

"Mom?" I began, taking care not to slur my words. "Mom, I just feel like I need to tell you . . . for no specific reason, but just because I really want you to know . . ."

I paused, hoping to draw her attention, but she didn't look up from her magazine.

"I just want you to know that . . . I really love you."

I moved myself so much with the power of my own emotions that my voice cracked slightly on the word "love," and actual tears started in the corners of my eyes.

Mom sighed but continued staring down at the pages in front of her. I assumed she was having an experience similar to mine.

"Having you," Mom said finally, her eyes on her magazine, her right hand turning the pages, "having you was the worst mistake I ever made in my life."

My vision tunneled, the blood roared in my ears, and I teetered. I was so shocked, so taken aback, that you could have knocked me over with a dish towel. I backed silently out of the kitchen and made my way upstairs in a sort of waking dream. I closed my bedroom door and sat on the edge of my bed. I felt like I couldn't catch my breath. I looked at the walls and the windows, those dumb barriers black with the night outside them, as if they could tell me something I needed to know. But they remained mute and indifferent.

So it was true. Mom had no use for me.

As much as this revelation anguished me, I also found it perversely validating. At least my perceptions were accurate: I was objectionable, but I wasn't crazy. Mom wasn't crazy either, although it might have been convenient to think so. She was sad, and her sadness made her mean, and I was unwise to expect anything from her except aggravation and grief.

All things considered, I shouldn't have been surprised. The mask was off, revealing the face that Mom had shown to me so many times. I'd like to be able to say that I had enough self-respect, enough of a sense of my own worth as a human being, to have shaken off the terrible barb that Mom had stuck in me, but it was not so. I told myself over and over that what Mom had said to me couldn't be true, but I believed it anyway. I couldn't say no.

I spent the rest of my time at home, until the day after my eighteenth birthday—and in some ways the rest of my life up until now—attempting to turn myself into a different person. Maybe I could change myself, or change the world, or change the relationship between myself and the world. I didn't know what that change would be nor how I could bring it about. But I determined, on that night in the summer of 1973, to do everything I could to make it happen.

—from Jonathan Weinert's unpublished memoir, *Five Minutes in Heaven*

Fiction

Patricia Foster

We Can't Save Them All, Can We?

1984

First, I hear loud knocking, then a wheezy voice. "Mrs. Connelly! Mrs. Connelly!"

I don't move. Outside the kitchen window, I see the bald head of Mr. Arnaud, our shrunken, mean-spirited neighbor, ready to spew his awful gossip. "Whore-bait!" he hisses whenever he spies a girl in short-shorts, a girl in a crop-top or a mini. Last June, he looked out his bedroom window to see Rachel sunbathing in her plum-colored bikini, soaking up the mid-day sun, and in minutes he stood at my door, his face lobster red, his mouth twitching. "I cannot allow—" he blustered, "—this . . . this . . ."

"Mrs. Connelly!" His voice is wobbly, but the knocking has stopped. Though last summer, I insisted Rachel sunbathe on the other side of the house, today I'm in no mood to be polite. I sit at my kitchen table with a tepid cup of tea in my old green mug. I don't remember making tea. I don't remember getting up from this chair in the last two days except to respond to the call of nature. When I glance at the counter, I see an empty milk carton, tilted on its side, its throat yanked open. There are plates full of crumbs littering the table. A glass half-full of water, two dirty coffee cups. Did I eat anything today? Yesterday? I don't remember. I remember only the useless calls from Sergeant Burkett at the police station, explaining something about shelters in Atlanta and New Orleans and Nashville.

Now I keep very still, hoping Mr. Arnaud will vanish into his white two-story house with its peeling green shutters, its dying asparagus ferns, its Reagan/Bush signs that still flag his yard. I wait ten minutes, then put down my mug and walk to the window, noticing for the first time that it's raining, a steady drizzle, the sky an anxious, blurry gray like an over-washed sheet. I watch Mr. Arnaud creeping back across his lawn. "Sir Lester Dedlock," Rachel calls him, after that witless snob in *Bleak House*. Mr. Arnaud gets in his old Buick and backs cautiously out of his straight, narrow driveway, *careful, careful*, until his right front tire sinks deep into his bed of pansies. *Again.*

I sigh. But it's a relief to notice other people's mistakes, a relief now that I know where Rachel is. *Is.* Present tense. Just thinking this, I feel a rush of warmth as if I've discovered a sixth sense, as if I'm linked to my daughter through the tiny hairs on my skin, the cells of my fingernails or through the waffles and omelets and popovers I've made for her throughout the years. *Do I really know where my daughter is?*

What happened is this: fifteen minutes ago, I picked up the ringing phone and heard Rachel's voice, raspy and thick with phlegm as if she had a bad cold. "Mom, it's me," she said as if she were calling from her friend Natalie's house and only wanted me to pick her up instead of being missing for two full days.

"Honey," I whispered, yanked fully into the present. "Oh, Rachel, for Godsakes, where are you?" And then I started crying even though I'd promised myself I wouldn't.

"I'm okay, Mom."

"What? Do you just *hate* me? Are you trying to punish—"

"*Mom!* I'm in New Orleans. I'm safe."

Safe. I thought of Patty Hearst, of kidnapping, violence, death, a gulping silence. I listened through the phone for noises in the background, for horns honking, the loud rustle of crowds, the screech of streetcars as I waited for Rachel to tell me exactly where she was. "Your father and I can be there in three hours," I said quickly. "You know that. Just give me an address."

"Mom, I need another day."

"You need to come home. You can't—"

"I'm hanging up now."

"Rachel, please . . ." I took a deep breath. I thought I might survive if I could just keep her on the phone. "Are you eating breakfast . . . at least tell me that."

"Oh, Mother, how silly."

"No, it's not silly. Breakfast is your foundation. It's—"

"I'm okay," Rachel repeated. And then she cleared her throat. "I just need another day here."

"Rachel?" To calm myself, I imagined two eggs frying in the skillet, the way I liked to fix them, the edges crisp and ruffled, the yolks yellow bleeding suns, two rounds of Canadian bacon already on her plate and a slice of fresh papaya.

"I'm hanging up now, Mother."

"Goddamit, Rachel. At least orange juice."

And to my surprise, she laughed, a sound I hadn't heard from her in months. "I'll call back in three hours."

Then the phone went dead though I kept talking, saying all the things I hadn't been able to say. "Rachel, tell me you're all right, tell me why you left, tell me where you are." I didn't say I haven't eaten or slept, haven't changed my clothes, or even brushed my teeth in two days. Who was there to hear?

When I hung up the phone, I knew I should immediately call the police, but I was carried by such a heightened awareness, the kind that says, "Be still. Don't react" that I sat down. *Don't be an idiot, Martha*, I could hear John saying. *She's 15. Call the damn police.*

But I didn't. It was as if a younger, happier Rachel was sitting across from me in her nightgown and fuzzy slippers, begging me to wait. *Please*, she kept saying, *it's important.* And so, I stepped outside of myself for a minute, trusting this feeling, abiding by something I couldn't yet name. That is, until Mr. Arnaud interrupted, getting between me and the feeling.

Now I'm trembling. I stare at the phone, tempted again to call the police, but instead of reaching for it, I move towards Rachel's room as if drawn by a palpable hope, drawn towards a door I haven't opened in two full days. Though I enter with trepidation as if frightened of the unknown, all I see is familiarity: Rachel's double bed with its bright floral spread, the pale pink comforter bunched up and pushed to the baseboard, her clothes dropped in puddles—jeans, t-shirts, underwear (I notice black cotton panties wadded up), shorts, even skirts strewn on the floor. A typewriter and books and papers stacked up on the desk, and inside that desk, I know, are hidden packages of cake doughnuts and Hersey bars and Fruit Loops and Cheese Curls. The closet door is left open, shoes thrown in higgly-piggly, a pair of swim goggles hanging mutinously from the door handle along with a clutch of rubber bands. A rectangular mirror covers the bathroom door. How often did my daughter sit in this bed and stare sullenly in that mirror, perhaps watching her body thicken and swell, her cheeks plump out, a girdle of fat circling her waist? How often did she munch on onion rings, barely conscious of the grease stains on her t-shirt and shorts as she watched her mouth open and close?

Two days ago, the police insisted we leave everything as it was, but now I step on a puddle of clothes and push aside the flowered spread, sinking into Rachel's bed like a thief while staring at my own disheveled self in the mirror: streaked hair falls into an awkward part, bangs split into little clumps, my sweater frumpy, stretched-looking, though it's practically brand new. But I don't really see myself, only my daughter dressed in those wretched clothes, the baggy pants she now prefers, the too-tight shirts and ratty tennis shoes, the ripe scent of sleep-smelly pajamas still clinging to her skin, and I wonder when exactly she ducked beneath my radar, slipped into shadow, hidden and plotting. I thought I was watching her so carefully, so closely.

As I lean back into Rachel's bed, untwisting the sheet and pulling the covers up over me as if I might get closer to her here, I surprise myself by thinking not about Rachel but about Denise Underwood and a day last year when two ninth graders rushed into my class, all breathless and excited, as if they had big news. "Wait till you *see* what Denise is wearing," they blurted, their voices rising. "You're gonna have a *fit*, Mrs. Connelly."

I knew better than to react. Girls that age are so scornful, so aggressively critical, flagellating themselves for the slightest nonconformity, I felt only a mild apprehension. All year Denise Underwood had worn loose, faded peasant dresses, old-fashioned and chaste, with scooped necks and twenty different colored buttons down the front. Dark-haired and voluptuous and depressed, she often slumped in her seat, was late with her lab reports, handing them in with messy erasures or tea-colored splotches as if carelessness was an aesthetic. I tried to help her, and if that was resisted, gave her the benefit of the doubt because her mother was dying of breast cancer and she and her two younger brothers were being raised by their father, Silas, one of the town's four policemen.

But that day when she walked into my class, my first response was surprise: *my God, she is beautiful! Why look at her!* She'd cut off her long ponytail and her dark hair swayed, thick and heavy, just above her shoulders. She stood straight and tall as if suddenly, this day, she meant to be noticed. And of course, she *would* be noticed in a white halter top exposing a smooth, tan stomach above tight black pants. Almost instantly, two of the more popular boys began teasing her about her notebook, yanking at it, goggling at her.

"Begin reviewing the Atomic Table for the next fifteen minutes," I said after calling the class to order. "I want you to know the names and symbols of the most common elements and the scientific names and chemical formulas for salt, baking soda and lime. And don't forget the test on Friday. *Everyone* will be tested, so no excuses." Then, quietly, I asked Denise to come out in the hall with me as if I had an errand in mind.

She stood nonchalantly, the smell of some flowery perfume surrounding her, her face bland, noncommittal but cautiously alert. I had to repress the instinct to smile. "Now Denise, I'm afraid you can't come to lab dressed like this."

Immediately, she stiffened, hardening her jaw. "Why can't I dress like this? My daddy saw me this morning and he didn't complain." There, she'd thrown down the gauntlet. Her father, the policeman, didn't complain.

"Denise, you look absolutely adorable . . ." I paused, feeling my way, "for the beach. But we're using acid and fire and glass today and what you're wearing is not appropriate for lab. I don't want you to get hurt, dear. Remember how we talked about protective clothing at the beginning of the year. You'll have to go to the office and see if your father can bring you some clothes. A long sleeve shirt, I think, will do."

She glared at me, eyes like fiery chestnuts, and then walked slowly, sullenly to the office.

Ten minutes later when Silas Underwood came to the school, he looked so surprised to see his daughter sitting defiantly in the principal's office in her sexy outfit that he stood in the doorway a moment, silent, blinking, undone. I'd come to meet him, to act as a referee if needed. I thought he'd be angry or embarrassed, that he'd snap at his daughter or rebuff her by quickly and silently handing over the clothes. But he did something that surprised me. He took a blue shirt out of a brown paper bag—what looked like one of his own work shirts—and very carefully, almost gracefully, draped it around her shoulders, hugging her to him, patting her back and saying, "It's okay, honey," in a voice so soothing, so loving, I had to look away.

When I told Rachel this story at dinner, she shook her head. "God, Mom," she shrieked, "You can't *do* that! You can't tell girls what they can and can't wear. Geez, you're acting like Sir Lester Deadhead next door. That's like, well, it's like fascism."

Rachel was slouching in her chair in one of her plaid skirts, one leg crossed over her knee, something white hanging out.

"Rachel, what's that under your skirt . . . is it—"

"Mom!"

"No, what *is* it?" I leaned closer.

Rachel uncrossed her leg and straightened in the chair. "It's Daddy's boxers, Mom. Jesus, all the girls in my grade are wearing them."

And despite myself, I laughed out loud. I might restrain the daughters of others, but I had no idea about my own. And that day I knew I had to notice Rachel in a different way. More than what she wore and said, I told myself to listen to her body's voice, to note the tensing of her shoulders, the quick dart of her hands, the sudden squinting of her eyes. When I quieted down, I swear there was a vibration, a hum, a kind of thrumming between us and I knew her mood, her temperament, sometimes even her decisions. "Martha, you've gone daffy," my friends said, laughing at me. "Don't be a looney. She'll outsmart you!" But when I was tuned in to Rachel—watching her expressions, her gestures—I thought I knew, even before she did, what she would do. I knew she'd quit the swim team. She didn't really like competitive sports, had been doing them mainly to please her father, had begun to slump at the breakfast table, to stare resentfully at the rolled up towels beside her books. Then, three weeks later she quit. And I knew she'd do something that frightened me, some insurrection, a hard, little slap at the status quo, a protest against what her father and I had become and what she assumed we wanted *her* to become. What I didn't know was how much she wanted to avoid being like *me.*

"I don't know what anything means," Rachel said to me one evening this fall when I came into her room to say good night. She sat up, clearly agitated, her hair clumped up in a tangled rubber band. "I go to bed every night in a double bed under a floral bedspread while other people live their lives in shacks with dirt floors and rats and no running water."

"It's definitely unfair," I agreed, but I was looking out the window at the darkening night, the sky a deep, lonely black. I listened to a branch scratching against the roof, a plaintive sound.

"That's all it is to you, isn't it?"

I glanced at her. "I grew up on Flat Top Hill, Rachel. Not exactly Bel Air."

"But you *got out.* What about the people who can't?"

"Well, I guess that's why I teach school. So, I can help other people find a way out."

"Oh, *Mo-ther*, there are people who don't even have a chance to *go* to school," she said impatiently as if I'd missed the point.

"I know that, Rachel. But we help those who can. We can't save the world. We save individuals, that's all."

She muttered "oh, *sure*," and wrapped herself up in her comforter as if I were irredeemable, a mother fundamentally flawed by her lack of compassion for the poor. "Find out everything you can, Rachel, before you condemn us all." And I walked out of her room.

But I had not walked out of the conversation.

Now as I lie in Rachel's bed, I feel the hard slap of uncertainty: what if my *not* telling Rachel about my past has made her see me as irrelevant, merely a doctor's wife, a science teacher, a privileged woman with a wallet full of credit cards? Whenever I talked about Flat Top Hill, I always made it comic and backwards, full of turnip greens and outhouses and torn rubber galoshes instead of the desperate, mean-spirited place that it was. I never told her about Tom Pettus or about that March night when I was 16 and the crucial decision I made about what kind of person I wanted to be.

Most particularly, I see how Mama—a card-carrying skeptic—sneered at Tom Pettus, the new minister's red-headed son who theatrically refused to wear a white shirt and tie to church like the other men, miners who understood that the good Lord deserved your best. Instead, he dressed in worker's denim, a faded but clean shirt and wrinkled jeans, his hair thick and curling over her collar. "Play-acting," Mama said with open disdain. "He'll need praying for soon."

But to me he looked alert and defiant, mocking the respectability we so desperately yearned for. I looked around at the shabbiness of our church, the smell of old leaves and must, the plain, polished pews and the plain, wiry men in starched shirts and faded ties and the wide-hipped women in soft, flowered dresses and then I sneaked a look at Tom Pettus. I liked the way he held the hymnal straight out in front of him even though he refused to sing certain songs because they suggested too easy a salvation.

Too easy a salvation! The audacity of it.

Well, I considered myself a fit match for anything Tom Pettus might throw my way. And so, I was surprised in the church basement that night—both of us assigned to put out cookies and lemonade for the parishioners—when he suggested I was "brainwashed" for saying Flat Top Hill wasn't so bad. "Already gone deaf and blind, huh," he smirked.

"Not blind," I said, staring at him. I noticed the rash of freckles crowded at the bridge of his nose.

He grinned and snapped a dish towel in the air, making a crackling sound. "Ever done anything you shouldn't?" he asked, leaning against the counter and pulling out a cigarette.

I didn't answer. I watched as he blew a stream of smoke into the air. I noticed how his gray eyes, large and thick-lashed, stared intently, even arrogantly, at me. "Well, from what I can see this place stinks."

I want to laugh now. Well, of course, it stunk, a mining town in the early 1940s crowded with poor, uneducated people, trapped in heavy-lidded grief and hardness, but when I was 16, it never occurred to me there was any option other than escape.

But Tom Pettus believed in something more radical than escape, and for a moment, I can see Rachel standing right beside him, shoulder to shoulder, her blue eyes filled with the same awed excitement, the same dismay. For months, I saw Tom only at church, which the Pettuses had painted a warm ivory on the inside, a surprise to the rest of us who had gotten used to the dark, faded gray, dreary but familiar. Often Tom and I would be together in the basement kitchen, where he'd push his hand in the soapy water while I was washing the coffee cups, and then, quite suddenly, he'd start ambushing me, flinging water at me so I'd have to chase him around the room. Or he'd bump into me, pretending to lose his balance, so that I dropped the forks and spoons I was drying.

What changed everything was a late February Sunday, a week after the miners had been forced to take a two-cent pay cut because of a lean season. Tom and I were making hot chocolate, boiling water in the big kettle on the stove for the night service. He always kept up some banter, mimicking Mr. Brewster gobbling up the chocolate cake or Mrs. Wiley pretending she didn't have a wad of snuff hidden in her cheek or Mr. Jawoksi's stuttered curses, "Ggggoodd-daaang!" But tonight, he was tense, furious, his face solemn and secretive. "Those men should *do* something," he said, pacing back and forth from the table to the window. He believed the miners should go on strike, just like the Pennsylvania miners had done in the Homestead Strike back in the 1890s, because without action—protests, picket lines, strikes—*the underdogs can't push against the bosses,* he always said. But our families were stoic; we knew to wait out trouble, adding a bit more water to the cornmeal, patching up last year's shoes, hardening our will.

I was flattered by Tom's attention, his ranting about unions and picketing as if *he* had every right to question the owners' decisions, as if the problem here was mainly a lack of anger. And maybe it was. Our daddies knew how the lines were drawn: they could bully and abuse their own, whipping and hectoring wives and kids, drinking up their wages, cheating Negroes and foreigners, but together they stood quiet and respectfully distant before their betters. "Silver tea service don't talk to the kettle," Mama would say.

"That company should belong to the people," Tom said, staring at me, "but the people have to demand what's theirs."

"Well, maybe someone should tell them," I said, trying to get back to our teasing ways. I dried the chipped cups and placed them upside down on the table. Of course, I didn't believe that anything would change here. No, the only thing that could be changed was my future. And that would be altered not by miners protesting on Flat Top Hill but by a scholarship to the university, something earned by brains and goodness: a girl who did nothing wrong, rocked no boats, cast no stones.

"Maybe," he said. I could feel him thinking, examining the thing, turning it this way and that in his mind. But just then the kettle whistled a long, hissing sound that startled us both so that we grabbed for it, our bodies colliding, his hips pressed against me, his hands covering mine as the kettle shrieked. "*I'm* going to do something," he whispered, and he leaned so close I was suddenly aware of his bare forearms, my rising breasts, and the thick, sweet smell of cocoa.

"Hey," someone yelled down the stairs. "What's going on?"

Tom jerked away while I turned off the stove and poured hot water into a pitcher of cocoa. I could feel his body, lingering and agitated, behind me.

That night, I lay in bed listening to the wind in the trees, but instead of thinking about college, I imagined running away with Tom Pettus, running away to New York or Chicago, to some dark, deviant city, flaunting the impossible, surviving on rebellious energy.

The next week, such a possibility arrived. Tom asked to walk me home after church on Sunday night and right after service, we met on the path outside the church lane, avoiding the muddy low spots, stepping carefully on the graveled bed. After gazing anxiously behind him, Tom confided that his father was pressuring him about college, even demanding the ministry. "The ministry," he laughed. "Those pious hypocrites. Old puffed up prudes. They sip brandy with the bosses."

I remember the cold air of late evening, the smell of sulfur mixed with the scent of cedars planted beside the church, the dark, somber path ahead of us. Fog circled the lights, swept low among the tree trunks. I pulled my jacket tighter to my chest, seeking warmth, watching the white clouds of breath as I exhaled. As we walked down the graveled road together, I felt suddenly free and hopeful and when Tom caught hold of my hand, I didn't pull away.

"I can't go to college yet," he said, smiling. "I've got *things to do.*" He raised his eyebrows, then pulled me closer. For a moment, we stood suspended, alone in the dark, his hand lifting the hair from my neck as he kissed a necklace around my throat. The pleasure of it burst through my blood, thrilling, and then scaring me. I pulled away. We walked on in silence for a few minutes until Tom stopped and said softly, "People shouldn't have to live this way." And before I could figure out what to say, he lifted my face and kissed me again, his tongue now alive in my mouth, touching my tongue and waking up sensations I hadn't even known were possible. "Come away with me," he whispered, his lips pressed into my hair. "Let's go to Pittsburgh," he said as if Pittsburgh carried some magical aura, some ardent freedom. "Just you and me. Let's show them anybody can leave." He kissed the side of my face, then looked up at the cold, wintry sky. "You can't stay here"—he kissed me again—"any more than I can. You're like me, more than you think." It wasn't a question. And as if something had been decided, he put his arm around me, hugging my shoulders, and then he grabbed my hand and kissed the inside of my wrist as if this was a newly precious spot—all the while talking about how we'd hitchhike north, staying with "the good people we'd meet along the way," then go to his Uncle Walt's in Pittsburgh, who would put us up and help us find work, and teach us how to outsmart the bosses. When he rested his hands on my shoulders, I could feel his breath again, warm and excited, electric in my hair. His plans seemed, in that moment, both utterly ridiculous and inevitable.

He said we should stay away from each other during the week, and then meet the next Sunday night at midnight at the cemetery.

By 10:00 p.m. on Sunday, I was all dressed for the trip to Pittsburgh—a long t-shirt, long johns and two sweaters, a skirt over a pair of pants, double pairs of socks, and thick gloves. From my bedroom window, I watched the snowflakes fall against the bare ground, watched the flocking of the bare limbs and the cradle of snow in the ditches.

I thought how Mama would be surprised when I left, how she'd see I wasn't so good and pliable after all, her rising star, steady and practical and predictable. But as I listened to the clock tick out the final minutes, I could not make my body move out of my room. I felt dazed and defenseless, my mind soft, gelatinous, until something hard-edged and decisive took over, something much more rebellious than the girl who meant to throw caution to the wind by running away. I didn't want to live in Pittsburgh or walk picket lines. I hated the underdogs. I hated the dull, damp rooms, the boiled potatoes and cabbage, the scrimping, the fighting. A selfish hunger flickered and blazed in me.

I wanted to escape, all right, to where there was light and beauty and air. I wanted that scholarship. I began peeling off all the layers of clothes, leaving on only the socks as I pulled the blankets tight over my head.

Remembering this, I jerk upright in Rachel's bed, pushing away the covers. I hadn't told Rachel about Tom Pettus because she'd see this as one more example of how I'd chosen myself, how I'd pushed and shoved to escape the very people she wanted to help. I wanted those credit cards, this pretty house with its Oriental rugs and chandeliers. If I told Rachel about Tom Pettus, then she'd know she was right: I didn't want to look where she looked.

I don't see the letter at first. Though I spent thirty minutes lying in Rachel's bed, I'm now looking across to Mr. Arnaud's house with the peeling green shutters. The rain has stopped. A honeysuckle vine grows over his porch with its lone metal glider. I imagine that's where Mr. Arnaud sits to spy on us, idling back and forth, one foot steady on the wooden floor. I open the back door, some premonition perhaps, though the intent seems sane enough: I want to get some fresh air. Anxiety clutches at my throat. What makes me glance down, I have no idea, but immediately, I notice a letter prominently placed on the doormat, facing me. The Masthead's a black-ribbon scribble: **Free South Africa Movement**. It is addressed to Miss Rachel Connelly but in the corner, I see Mr. Arnaud's scrawl: *This was misdelivered to my address*. And then a single slander: *Communists!*

Looking at that word, I start to tremble. I'm not of Mr. Arnaud's persuasion but I'm shocked that Rachel's name appears on the address. How did it get there? When I open the letter, I see it's a flier announcing an Anti-Apartheid rally in New Orleans. The drawing is crude—

no hammers and sickles—but black men chained together, their faces contorted in a rictus of agony. It's a bad photocopy, some of the figures blurry with dots, others merely dark smudges. At first, I think police. I think *call John*. I think, oh, Rachel, what are you involved in? Who are these people? But then, another thought gets hold of me, another memory sweeps through my brain as if it's just been waiting to appear: it is the day Silas Underwood came to see me not long after the incident of his daughter, Denise's white middy top. I was tidying up the lab, organizing papers, and when I looked up, he stood at the classroom door, a large but quiet presence, a man in his policeman's uniform, his hat off, his gun at his hip. He came, of course, to talk about Denise. He was shy at first, coming only two steps further into the room and then standing formally though I wanted him to sit down and feel comfortable. But no, he said. He wanted only a minute.

"Her mother," he said softly, glancing shyly at me, "well, you see, her mother had to let go her hand." He looked exhausted, dark circles shadowing his eyes. He spoke slowly, tentatively. "And now Denise has got, well, Mrs. Connelly, she's gotta find her own way."

I nodded. And yet what I saw was myself standing at my old bedroom window, watching the softly falling snow and knowing I wouldn't follow Tom Pettus to Pittsburgh, wouldn't forsake my ambition for his, and yet not ready to take off my double pair of socks.

"She's just trying to say she's still alive, Mrs. Connelly," he said. He looked gently at me then as if I might not understand, and I felt startled and moved. Moved because I saw what a good man he was, a man who understood his daughter's anguish, recognized her most urgent desires, the ones not yet expressed but still floating in darkness. "It will likely take some time."

I wanted to reach out and touch him.

Now I think of Silas Underwood as I stare at the flier. *Still alive*.

Not long after I talked with Silas Understood, Denise brought a camping knife to school one day and though she only showed it to a few girls in the Girls' Bathroom, she told them she brought it "to cut the gizzard out of Kenny Johnson," an older boy who had snatched her purse in class, opened it and showed everyone her Tampax. She'd been suspended for having a knife at school, but even accepting her punishment, she looked satisfied, triumphant. I watched that day as she walked out of the principal's office, her head held high, her gaze clear and undefended. She'd fought back. She'd insisted that what was hers was private and valuable, not to be messed with. When she came to school the next week, she seemed both quieter and more confident. She turned in her homework, still messy, and put her pencils in a new green purse.

I turn the flier over and stare at Rachel's name. I make myself breathe slowly, in and out. Rachel. I see my daughter marching through the streets of New Orleans, her ugly shirt too tight, her messy hair coming loose from its ponytail, her ordinary teenage life, so full of helpless anger, temporarily suspended as she walks, chanting with the others, breathing in unity and hope while the black men, chained together in another country, struggle for release.

I fold the flier and put it in my pocket. And then I walk back into the kitchen and break two eggs in a skillet, mixing in some grated cheese and diced peppers, and getting out the Canadian bacon to fry while I wait for my daughter to call.

Nathan Alling Long

Evelyn Dorsett on the Fence

She does this every chance she can, all through the summer, for hours on end, sits on the fence near the tracks, waiting for the train, the roar of its engine and the thick black smoke, the horn that shakes her bones and smarts her ears. She loves how it rattles every cell in her body, shakes her free like a shaft of late summer wheat, every grain dropping to the ground, scattered, so that what seemed like a certain tight bundle of grains, smooth and pressed, pointing toward the sky, becomes nothing more than a shadow, a memory, a watercolor image, washed away by the heavy dense mass of cars as they pass before her.

Even if there is no train in sight, she sits on the fence, even when it is hot, or windy, or on those rare cold summer afternoons when the sky darkens with angry clouds and the wind pulls off ripe green leaves from the trees and spins them in the air like lost birds and everything in the field and woods seems to scatter, to take shelter, when even the air tries to make itself scarce, and she has to take deep breaths just to fill her lungs and not feel a little light headed and empty.

In fact, that is her favorite moment to sit on the fence, when the world seems to swirl around her, as though she is in the midst of an enormous change of scenery on the stage and everyone is too busy taking out one set of props and replacing them with another, lowering the new backdrop before getting off stage, to even notice that she is sitting right there in the middle of it all.

Today is one of those rare afternoons, when the horizon is so dark, she can almost imagine that the storm approaching is the night rushing in, hurried and apologetic, throwing its overcoat and hat and scarf over the bright blue sky and pretending that its heart is not beating fast from the rush. She does not care now if a train comes at all. The sky is enough.

And when the sky is all a roar and the wind is full of the scent of a hundred plants, when leaves and petals and dust and specks of who knows what are swirling around her, when the sky is roiling like a boiling pot of some dark witches' brew and she can hear the scattering of brush animals and insects, the caw and flap of birds as they try to escape the massive ship that is plowing toward them from the horizon, then it takes every tinsel of concentration for Evelyn to stay steady on the rail, to not waiver and fall off, to counterbalance against the constantly shifting wind, to press both hands into the wood to steady herself.

It is as though, sitting there on the fence—neither on the ground not in the air, neither in her home nor in town—Evelyn is no longer herself, no longer part of her upbringing and all that makes her human. She becomes simply one of the crickets burrowing beneath a thicket of grass, or a starling darting into the bush, or a mole scurrying down deep underground. Her hair whips free, strands tossed across her face and neck, as though she were a tree whose branches are thrown back and forth, a bush shaken of loose leaves, the field of grass more conduit of wave than solitaire stalk.

She feels such swirling within her now, her molecules realigned by the sweep of the natural world, into some version of herself she has known since birth, or before birth—a self that has no words to it, that becomes mute in the presence of language, a self that can only be found alone in a field or under a tree, or here on the fence, a self that is more sturdy than the self who answers to Evelyn, because it has no weight of its own.

And to even hear the far-off moan of the train horn now sends new shivers up her ribs and into her chest, unwraps her, undoes her. There in the storm, as she feels the locomotive churning toward her, she is reminded of that other force that she is in some reluctant way a part of, the force of all human beings, of all they bring—something massive, unwavering, inflexible, and violent in its determination and direction, unyielding to any other force.

And as the train nears, drawing to her the thunder and dark clouds, as though it could haul a storm the size of the sky in its tiny coal cars, Evelyn's body shakes on the edge of the rail. Faintly, above the clack and churn of the locomotive's wheels, she hears her mother's voice, calling her name. But she is no longer that name. She is already nothing at all.

The engine is upon her. Behind her, the wind turns and picks up force. The first drops of rain patter around her. She cannot keep things together. Her hands let go. Inside, she shatters like the glass jar she once dropped on the porch steps, like the thin ice she steps on in the early winter puddles, like the porcelain doll's head left on the lane and accidentally run over by a truck tire.

Nadeem Zaman

The Holy Visit

He was coming to Chicago for three days at the end of the month and Minnie Azad volunteered to host him. Volunteer was not the right word. Minnie had prayed for the opportunity. It was here and she was grabbing it.

"Minnie, you know how much he wants, right?" said Taslima Ahsan. Taslima was head of the committee overseeing arrangements for the visit, although, in light of certain developments of late, was reconsidering the position. "And, Minnie, those nasty, awful things that have been going around about him. I don't know what to think."

"It will not be enough for me to just see him from a distance with a crowd around me," Minnie said. "Or at someone's house I don't like. And you know who's saying nasty, awful things? Nasty, awful people. I can't believe you pay such nonsense any mind."

"I'm only saying, oh God, Minnie, calm down. I don't pay them any mind. Me and Faruk, we send him money too. But twenty thousand, Minnie, is out of our reach."

"Who is telling you to reach?"

Taslima looked around at the three other women in her living room.

"Did I say I want help?" Minnie said. "You all do your part, I'll do mine. Once the date is set, let me know."

"That man is a shady character not of today," said Mustafa Azad. "His whole family is. Only other nutjobs and cranks fall at their feet."

"Including me, right?" Minnie held the teacup halfway to her mouth and stared at her husband. "You know, sometimes it's enough to just let things be. People's beliefs are their beliefs."

Minnie's eyes settled on the framed pictures on the sideboard.

"Okay," said Mustafa.

"Not everything has to take the brunt of your ridicule," Minnie said. "He's going to come here and he's going to connect me to my son."

"Minnie, darling—"

"Don't do that. I will go to the bank tomorrow." Minnie got up with her cup of tea and took Mustafa's empty one from the coffee table.

"Don't go into the accounts and do any funny business tonight."

"The bank? Funny business?" said Mustafa.

"Yes. No free lunch, right? That's what you say, isn't it? Why should he not get paid like anyone else for what he does?"

Mustafa watched her leave, then slowly made his way to the kitchen.

"How much?"

"No amount is too much. It's my money, too. That man will come here."

"Minnie, dear—"

"It's my money, too," Minnie said with finality. "Half my life I worked and saved. I will spend what is mine as I wish."

His name was Al-Hajj Mohammad Jafruddin, but he was known as Pir Baba to his followers as his father before him was called Boro Baba and his grandfather before that was Haji Baba. Generations of families had laid their hopes and dreams at their feet, lived and died by their blessings, and in many cases sold every last thing of value to donate to their holy coffers.

Pir Baba's family claimed their heritage from a line of Sufi saints that had settled in Bengal sometime in the thirteenth century, and in Bangladesh their blessings were sought by millions. Pir Baba lived in a new high-rise built on the location of his ancestral home in Old Dhaka, which he had sold to developers for a handsome fortune.

The lavish apartment was fitted with state-of-the-art technology and flat-screen TVs in every room. He had a fleet of cars, and drivers that lived in the building. Among his friends were some of the wealthiest men in the country, and politicians often sought his guidance. Army generals lunched with him and shared their dreams of coups to set the country straight again. The Prime Minister, too, had paid him visits, or had him visit her at the official residence, before the religious right that condemned men like Pir Baba for blasphemers expressed concerns and she had to change her mind.

For his visitors, Pir Baba kept a separate meeting place. It was the house of a man whose family Pir Baba's grandfather had saved from Hindu mobs in the final days of the British Raj. The man was long gone, and his descendants were happier taking Pir Baba's generous offer and moving on to better dwellings than wasting away in the crumbling old hull. The house had been in a state of slow decay for years. It served Pir

Baba's purpose nicely, showing his followers his humility despite his divine powers and grace, despite the providence bestowed on him through his complete devotion to God.

Recently, however, several former devotees had come forward with allegations of sexual misconduct. The women were derided. Pir Baba had gone on the record shedding tears and calling for God's thunder to smite him if their allegations were true. A young journalist interviewed the women and published their accounts. More women came forward. In the month following the publication of the report, a dozen women reached out to the journalist. She verified their accounts individually and found them both authentic and consistent. Each woman, of her own volition, swore they had not shared their accounts with each other. They'd all served Pir Baba separately at different times.

His supporters around the country showed their backing in legion. Mullahs gave Friday sermons calling the allegations hearsay. Even the imams that were not keen on men like Pir Baba, censuring them as one notch above apostates, stood with him, and went so far as to malign the women that had brought the charges against him. If it was him now, they claimed, tomorrow it would be one of them. That was where Bangladesh was headed. First, men of God would be targeted, then Islam itself would be attacked. The generals and the politicians, certainly the PM, all stayed clear of the fray. Finding the time optimal for his yearly trip abroad, Pir Baba left for his annual tour of the UK and US.

On previous trips, Pir Baba visited all the major cities except Chicago. Minnie spoke with envy with friends and relatives in New York and Philadelphia and Los Angeles, and wondered that he had even made a stop at a godforsaken place like Lincoln, Nebraska.

"They have Bangladeshis there?" she'd said.

Mustafa had laughed. "It's where INS used to process immigration applications, of course they're there. Idiots probably thought it would jump them ahead in the cue."

Work had kept Minnie from planning a trip to one of the other cities to coincide with Pir Baba's visit, but after Ashraf died and she retired, meeting the holy man became a quest.

"But no," she'd maintained, "I will not go to Bangladesh to do it. I don't want those bad memories cursing it."

Minnie's father, two brothers, and an uncle had been killed by the

Pakistan army during the war of liberation in 1971. Mustafa, too, had lost family members, but he still felt a deeper connection to Bangladesh than Minnie, though he had only gone back a handful of times since they migrated to the US almost fifty years ago.

Once Ashraf was in high school and the two older boys in and out of college and on to jobs, marriage, and family, Minnie began softening about Bangladesh, largely because of Ashraf. He wanted to visit. Mother and son made plans, and Ashraf started saving money. He ran a web design business alongside his job that had come out of an internship with a tech company the summer before senior year of high school. Minnie told him he didn't have to worry about the money, but Ashraf kept on saving. By the time of his death he'd saved close to five thousand dollars. And his death sent Minnie back to her reservations about Bangladesh.

"What does the country have to do with it?" Mustafa had said.

"It's cursed," Minnie returned to her former stance. "It took one family from me and wants to take the other."

"Minnie," said Mustafa setting down a glass of warm milk on her nightstand. "Just listen to me, please. Twenty thousand dollars. It's your money, too, yes, but it's money that took years of both of our lives to save. What would we do if something happened? Go back to work at our age?"

"You are such a drama queen," said Minnie, taking a sip of milk. "Just say what you want to say."

"You know what it is," said Mustafa. "This man is not your direct connection to God."

"Then that's what you believe."

"It's true."

"You believe things that I don't belittle. You thought George Bush was a good man, and then look what he did to Muslims for a hundred years in this country."

"Minnie, please think about this," said Mustafa. "I'm begging you."

"I have," said Minnie. "My mind is set."

"What about the allegations about him?"

"Those women should be slapped. They didn't get what they wanted, so they fling mud at a good man's reputation."

"No, Minnie, you don't believe that."

"I believe what I believe."

The next morning Minnie arrived at the bank ten minutes before they opened. She sat in the car facing east while she waited. The rising sun was Ashraf, telling her every morning he was okay, that his drowning was not her fault, that as long as the world existed and rotated, he would visit her every day.

At nine she entered the bank and went up to the teller counter.

"Twenty-thousand in cash?" said the skinny, goateed teller. Minnie's eyes teared up from his cologne.

"I'm in a hurry," said Minnie.

The teller said the transaction required the manager's override.

While Minnie waited, and the line behind her extended nearly to the door, with only one other teller working besides the one helping her, she saw in her mind Pir Baba arriving at her house. Minnie shook off thoughts of thinking him good-looking, with his glowing skin, deep brown eyes, wavy black-and-white hair, and hennaed beard. That solid mark of prayer on his forehead. She could see how women could find him attractive, his authority magnetic. Minnie had lost count of the times men had made passes at her, a comment here, a flirtatious remark there, but for heaven's sake, she didn't feel she was violated in any way, and God knew it was not cause to kill a man's name.

"Ma'am?" the teller was back, and with him was the manager, a plump Korean woman in her thirties with thick glasses and a lisp. One collar was tucked under the neck of her shirt. Her eyes were red, her nostrils raw, and she looked tired.

"Come with me, please?" the manager said.

"You know, I didn't come here to be stuck all day," Minnie said following her to her office.

"I understand," said the manager. "Just because of the amount, we need to fill out a few forms. You'll be on your way in no time."

While the manager waited for the forms to print, she said, "So, big plans?"

"No," Minnie said. She was looking at the line of framed pictures on the file cabinet behind the manager's chair, all of them of the manager and a white man Minnie guessed was her husband.

"I have to get rid of those," the manager said catching Minnie's eyes. "We just got divorced."

Minnie settled her hands on her purse and turned her attention to the sheets dripping line-by-line out of the printer. Ashraf would point out that the manager needed an upgrade.

"Do you have far to go?" the manager asked setting the documents in front of Minnie.

"What?"

"From here, today? Do you have far to go? That's a lot of money to carry on your person."

"I'm fine."

"I'm sure you'll be careful." Dimples pocked her cheeks as she tried for a smile.

"Is this it?" said Minnie signing the last of the documents.

"This is it." The manager went through the pages one more time, initialing and signing herself. "You can just go see Rakesh again. He should have the money ready for you."

The two stacks of cash were in a rubber currency bag with a zipper and no lock. Minnie almost asked Rakesh if he would walk with her to her car but felt silly and changed her mind.

In the car, Minnie put the bag in her purse and set the purse on the passenger seat. A moment later, she placed it on the floor, then, after a pause, slid it under the seat. She had a ten-minute ride home, for heaven's sake. That manager was paid to be paranoid.

Minnie started the car and jumped at the knocks on her window.

Rakesh's gaunt, hollow-cheeked face was almost pasted to the glass.

"Yes?" Minnie said rolling the window down. A blast of his cologne drew tears out of her eyes again.

"You forgot this," said Rakesh holding Minnie's driver's license.

"Oh." Minnie took the license. "How old are you?"

Rakesh stared at her.

"Why?"

"Young man, I'm old enough to be your mother and I asked you a simple question. You can be respectful."

"Twenty-two."

One year younger than Ashraf would have been.

"Okay," said Minnie. "But don't do that again."

"Do what?"

"Startle people like that. It's not nice."

Ashraf loved water. He loved it more than other kids his age. He was swimming laps by the time he was ten, not wanting to splash around in the kiddie pool with floats and inflated toys. He swam three to four times a week through junior high and high. It was unbelievable that an excellent swimmer like him would drown, in the shallowest end of Lake Michigan, just like that.

So what, it was December? The day was sunny, warm, fifty-five degrees. Ashraf wasn't the only person out there. There were people all over, jogging in shorts and tank-tops.

Ashraf was found against the rocks face down, fully clothed. It was ruled a suicide. No one saw the first sign, Minnie told the counselor she and Mustafa saw for a few months. More times than not, the counselor told them, there were none.

"Was he taking his medication regularly?" the counselor asked after learning of Ashraf's mental health history.

"No," said Mustafa. "It was the one thing he was bad about."

"They killed his appetite," Minnie said. "He felt horrible with all that bad weight gain."

Ashraf went to the lake year-round, day and night, up by Evanston and Northwestern University because he liked sitting on the rocks there. He cringed at the thought of swimming in it, though. The lakefront up and down the coast of Chicago, maybe with the exception of North Avenue beach, where the water was still too cold, was not the best for swimming. Ashraf sat by the water sometimes for hours. And if he went for a bite to eat or met up with friends for a late movie on the weekends, he texted both his parents.

Besides his work colleagues and a small circle of friends he'd had since the first grade, Ashraf kept a distance from people. He didn't date, didn't ask anyone out, even though his tendency to look brooding, disaffected, and walk around as though the world would never be stimulating enough brought him his share of flirtation. Swimming had made him broad-shouldered and lean, and his facial hair grew coarse and thick from an early age, which he kept in a perpetual shadow, adding to the look of walking under heavy storm clouds all the time.

That day there'd been no word from Ashraf late into the night and he hadn't texted once. Minnie called the friends he usually went out with, but none of them had heard from him. They filed a missing person's report. It didn't take long for the police to find Ashraf at the likeliest place they were told they could begin their search.

At night, Minnie heard sounds that woke her. Sometimes, in the middle of the day, they stilled her mid-step. Ashraf's room stayed locked except for the once-weekly dusting and vacuuming Minnie gave it. At those times, when she heard a creak in the floorboard, a closet hinge whine, she pressed her ear to the door and held her breath.

After her father and brothers were killed, Minnie's mother walked the house all night. She kept the windows on all three floors open, so when they returned to tell her they were at peace where they were, they could get in. One night Minnie heard her talking. She believed it was her mother getting her closure.

Ashik, Minnie and Mustafa's middle son, was at the house when Minnie came home. A warm fist of anger tightened in Minnie's stomach as she pulled into the driveway behind Ashik's car. The car was so old it had its own odor, the car equivalent of an unwashed body in sweaty clothes. It was leaking, too. A long, thin finger of oil oozing from under the car and trickling for the grass. Minnie smudged the tip of the leak with her foot like squashing a bug. She took off her shoes on the front stoop and left them outside.

Mustafa and Ashik were talking in low voices in the living room. They stopped as soon as Minnie opened the door.

"Don't stop on my account," Minnie said.

"Mom," Ashik came bustling out. He didn't look much better than his car and reeked of cigarettes. "You drove around by yourself with all that money?"

Mustafa was the worst when it came to keeping something confidential. Minnie would bet that he was on the phone with their sons the moment she was out the door. Asif, their eldest, thank God, had better things to do, like a job and a family, a wife that he was still with and children that weren't hateful of both parents. Ashik's estranged wife, angry daughter, and delinquency with alimony and child support had drained Minnie and Mustafa more than it had cost him, and there were still two years left before the child turned eighteen. It was also true that had it been any other reason than money, Ashik's scent, or cigarette fumes, would be nowhere to be found.

"I'm fine," Minnie said.

"Everything was fine?" said Mustafa, peeking his head into the hallway.

"No, I was held at gunpoint by highway robbers. For God's sake, you two," said Minnie. "Here," she held up the bag of money. "Happy?"

"Mom, you're just going to hand that guy all that money?" said Ashik.

Minnie held the bag tightly to her chest as Ashik's eyes fixed on it.

"How long has it been now, five months, since you were last here?" she said.

"If you want to just throw that money away, why not start a college fund for Naila?" said Ashik.

"That girl? College? With her mother's brain in her head?"

"Minnie, please," said Mustafa.

Minnie came back down the three steps.

"And who would be in charge of this fund?" she asked. "Her father?"

"You trust a con man more than your son?" said Ashik.

"What's the difference?"

"Minnie," said Mustafa.

"You need to get that poison-leaker out of my driveway," Minnie said, and went back up the stairs.

"Mom," Ashik went after her. Minnie locked her bedroom door and placed the bag of money in her closet. "Ashraf killed himself. He was depressed. He was sick. You can be angry at everyone forever, but it was no one's fault. Go throw two-*hundred*-thousand dollars on a swindler if you want. Ashraf isn't coming back."

Mustafa pulled Ashik away and took him downstairs. Minnie stayed in the bedroom until she heard the juddering turn of Ashik's engine and the long, tortured scream of a frayed belt. She came out only after its roar had faded in the distance.

When Asif showed up a couple of days later, tired, and slightly irritated, Minnie threw up her hands.

"You all," she said. "I worked and I raised you three. It's your father that's losing his mind, sitting around nagging like a village hag all day."

"It's okay, Mom," said Asif.

As a child, he had a habit of clenching his fists when he was stressed or upset. As an adult, it had become a part of him like breathing or scratching an itch. He had returned early that morning from a work trip and come over straight from the airport. His suit was crumpled, his eyes bloodshot.

"You know Ashik," he said, "if there's money in the air, he becomes a bloodhound."

"I knew at least you would see the sense," said Minnie.

"I don't know," said Asif. "Twenty-thousand dollars? For what? And you have to feed him and whoever comes with him, too."

"That's just plain courtesy," said Minnie. "I'm having other guests too. People I know in this town that also want to see him."

"Sounds like a lot," said Asif.

"I've invited only a certain number."

"When is this guy coming?"

"Don't call him 'this guy'. He will be here in two weeks."

"It's your money," Asif said, including his father. "It's no one else's business."

"He's not a good character," said Mustafa.

"Who is," Asif sighed. He yawned and rubbed his eyes. "You know what I have to start my day with today? Laying off fifty people. Because the merger I just helped my company with requires it. Does that make me a good character?"

"It's not the same," said Mustafa. "This man has charges of sexual assault. No, not the same."

"Then why isn't he in jail?" Minnie said.

"Because, Minnie, you know how these things go. One, it's Bangladesh, two, he's a powerful man."

"If he was guilty, he wouldn't be traveling around," said Minnie.

"That's just why he's doing it. To run."

"I will not tolerate this," Minnie said.

Asif looked at Mustafa.

"Is there somewhere else he's going where you can go and meet him?" he said.

"He is going to come to this house," Minnie said. "That is my final decision."

"Okay," Asif said, as if from a hundred miles away. "That's that."

The buzzing of the phone startled Minnie awake. Mustafa wasn't next to her. He'd gone to the den to watch TV after dinner, probably had fallen asleep.

"Mom, you have to listen to me," Ashik slurred. "This guy is a rapist and a crook. You can't just hand him twenty thousand dollars like a handkerchief for blowing his nose. Mom, I've been asking you and Dad for a year for help now while I get back on my feet."

"I was asleep, Ashik."

"I wish I could sleep."

"You can. Just put away the drink and close your eyes."

"Mom," Ashik's voice broke. "My house will be foreclosed at the end of the month."

"You don't need that big house to yourself anyway. Get a small apartment. Go back to your job. They didn't fire you, but you have to prove yourself again. Clean up. Pride gets us nothing."

"I'm your son."

"Go to sleep, Ashik."

"Fuck you."

Minnie ended the call. She turned her phone off.

The truth that anyone with the smallest amount of power had enemies was truer a hundred times over in Bangladesh. As Minnie saw it, that was what had happened with Pir Baba. She'd seen it happen to her own family. Good people, honest people, people with nothing but the good graces of their family and friends, brought down overnight by one poisonous word, one drop of fuel on a non-existent flame that then wrecked and razed their lives.

The night the Pakistan army took away her father and brothers and uncle, they'd initially gone to the neighbor's house following a lead that Bengali pro-independence fighters were keeping weapons buried in their yard. The neighbors might have been threatened, forced to give the army something to save their lives. It was never found out what drove them to send the army to Minnie's house because they'd moved away within days of the war's end. In those last days of the conflict, the army's desperation had reached a high that had turned it blind. They were stopping at nothing to root out sympathizers with the pro-independence movement. Minnie's father was involved in the Communist party in the British era, and he had served briefly in the United Front in the fifties. Twenty years later, he was still a well-known and respected figure. People in the neighborhood knew who he was, and not all of them were admirers. A little resentment was all it took sometimes.

There were countless holy men doing God-knew-what with young girls all over Bangladesh every day. The mullahs at the mosques that derided women as unholy vamps and unclean temptresses and then went home to underage brides, sometimes more than one, they took those children in the presence of their congregations with the consent of the girls' parents. They called it an offering to God, they called it God's will. They would never see a moment's ire, never suffer assaults on their good names, because they were doing their deeds with divine approval. Pir Baba, whose family had for generations devoted themselves to service, donated money, built schools and orphanages, spoken for peace across the faiths, and given thousands hope, haven, and healing, Pir Baba was the man they were out to ruin.

Minnie thought about what she could do for Pir Baba. Everyone always took from him, wanted him to give and keep on giving without considering how they might serve him too, return even a fraction of the comfort he brought them. Money wasn't everything. Money came and went. But a person had only one reputation.

Minnie was going to open her house to him, take him for who he was, show his life the respect it deserved.

Two days after Ashik's nighttime rant, Cheryl, for the first time ever, called her mother-in-law, a relationship she knew Minnie no longer acknowledged.

Cheryl had taken an active dislike to Minnie the moment they met because Minnie had said something to Ashik in Bangla that Cheryl had taken as being about her, then deciding that it was something bad. It was neither, and later Minnie didn't even remember what she'd said. After that Ashik groused every time Minnie spoke Bangla when Cheryl was around, even if she was on a different floor and out of earshot. He said it bothered her no less.

"Then that's on her, isn't it?" Minnie had finally said. "She shouldn't have married a Bangladeshi if she doesn't want to hear Bangla once in a while."

Cheryl's parents, too, were distant, aloof. Minnie told Mustafa not to try so hard but it was ingrained in Mustafa to fall all over himself around white people, just as his father had fawned over the British. Minnie's father had been a civil servant under the British, too, but, Minnie maintained, knew he was no less than any Englishman and held his head high.

"They're our in-laws, Minnie."

"Which Bangladeshi in-laws do you see worshipping each other? If these people don't like the man their own daughter chose, they can take it up with her."

Minnie was not heartbroken over the strained relations. Cheryl's parents never left their backwater town until their trip to Chicago for Cheryl and Ashik's wedding. They didn't seem any more interested in their new son-in-law's heritage than their daughter, or the world beyond their door for that matter. They were often rude to Naila and treated her like a stranger's child. Minnie didn't need to ask if they'd ever consider going to Bangladesh. Of course, Mustafa had to.

"Who knows," had been Cheryl's father's reply.

"I don't much like planes," said his wife.

Minnie was ten minutes late to their meeting on purpose, and she wished she'd made it double that. Cheryl was chronically late to everything Minnie invited them to when Cheryl and Ashik were still together, and Minnie always suspected it was on purpose. She waved to Minnie from a booth near the back of the café. She even got up and gave Minnie a hug. She reeked of cigarettes.

"I know we've never been in love with each other," she said. "So, thank you for meeting me. Your son told me about your conversation."

Conversation? That was their idea of a conversation?

"Naila is already excited about college," Cheryl said, trying to add cheer to her tone. "A parent's dream, right?" She smiled, showing a blackened incisor. "Anyway, Ashik said he spoke to you about a college fund, maybe?"

Cheryl brought her eyes up for a second. They dropped before Minnie could meet them.

"He just said," Cheryl went on, "that you and Mustafa were setting some money aside for, I don't know, he didn't specify really." She paused, took a sip of coffee with a loud slurp. "You know we're going to lose the house, right?"

"He mentioned," said Minnie. "So, you're back together?"

"No," said Cheryl, and left it at that. "Unless we come up with at least the amount of the down payment." She shot Minnie another look. "Twenty thousand."

Minnie wondered how profoundly dumb this woman and her own son thought she was. If they owed twenty thousand dollars' worth of mortgage payments they'd be thrown out long ago. And how convenient. Exactly twenty thousand. Minnie was sure they'd paid a different sum than that for a down payment.

"He's looking for work," Cheryl added. "He is."

Work, as opposed to a job, Minnie thought. Someone with a degree from one of the best universities in the country, an honors graduate, is looking for work—not a career. Someone who put in ten years at Sony America and another five with GM was looking for work like the favor-seekers that used to come begging Minnie's father for whatever scrap he could throw their way. Twenty thousand dollars would have dropped out of Ashik's pocket and forgotten by the end of the day once upon a time. And they did, drop out, by his own stupidity, over and over for all the wrong things, and now he was at this point, abusing his mother in the middle of the night drunk, and sending his wife who didn't want to be with him to clean up a grown man's mess.

"I don't know where," Cheryl said, "but that's the one thing about Ash, he's not a quitter. You guys raised him with all those good values you have back in Bangladesh."

She always said it like that. Back in Bangladesh. Like it was another planet.

"I guess, Minnie, what I'm saying is, he's right. And believe me, I haven't said those words in recent memory. Ash has been wrong for so long he thinks it's right. But about this, I agree. If you won't think of us, think of Naila."

"Cheryl," said Minnie, "I also raised my son with my values from back in Bangladesh to respect his mother and speak for himself. Remind him that." And, for the record, Minnie would have put twice as much into a college fund for Naila if she had any guarantee that Naila's feckless parents wouldn't pounce on it as soon as the money was in the bank.

Minnie brought out her purse.

"Do give my love to Naila," she said. "I would love to hear from her."

She placed a twenty on the table.

"Don't get up."

From her car she saw Cheryl look around, look over her shoulder, throw a glance out the window, then pick up the twenty and slide out of the booth.

"Minnie, wake up."

Minnie's eyes adjusted to the outline of Mustafa's head, shaggy with tousled hair.

"You were talking. To Ashraf."

"I was dreaming about him and me, together in Dhaka."

"Do you want a glass of water?"

"No."

Mustafa lay back down and put his arm over his eyes.

"You don't think twenty thousand dollars is a small amount to reach him? Just one more time?" said Minnie.

"I don't know," said Mustafa. "I really don't know, Minnie."

"If I could just know why," said Minnie.

"He was ill, Minnie. He didn't take his medication regularly."

"They made it worse."

"I don't know what to say anymore."

"No one does. Which is why I need Pir Baba."

"So now you've both lost your mind," said Ashik. "Cheryl tries to talk to Mom about Naila, her own granddaughter, and Mom treats her like shit. And now you, Dad. This fucking mullah's turned both your brains to dung."

"Ashik, stop," said Mustafa.

"Asif bhai? You have nothing else to say?" Ashik turned to his brother.

"This is not your house to throw around your tantrums. Not anymore," said Minnie.

"Asif bhai, will you say something?" said Ashik.

"You both should leave," said Mustafa.

"You know what," said Ashik, "I'm going to be here when this fraud humiliates you in front of everyone. Oh yes." Ashik crushed the cigarette he was smoking in an ashtray and slammed the front door behind him.

"Is he in danger or something?" said Mustafa. "Like gambling debts? He's desperate it seems."

"Probably not," Asif said flatly. "That's too sophisticated for him. I'll bet my house it's Cheryl, and it's probably with good reason."

"That woman ruined whatever good was left in him," said Minnie.

"Probably not," said Asif. "Dad, what changed your mind about this person?"

"It's what your mother wants," said Mustafa.

Asif sat back, took a sip of his tea, and set down the cup.

"Sarah wants to come, too," he said. "Mom?"

If Cheryl was the daughter-in-law that didn't care to like Minnie or be liked by her, Sarah was the one that tried too hard.

"That's fine," Minnie said.

The morning of Pir Baba's visit, Minnie woke up at four and cleaned the house all over again, the two hours she'd spent cleaning the night before no longer enough. She burned incense and spread a white sheet on the floor of the living room, the way her mother would for Eid prayers at the house. She sprinkled rose water on the sheets, and at nine the refreshments were delivered. Gafoor, the owner of the restaurant, knew about Pir Baba, and offered money for a prayer to be said for his wife. She was ill. Minnie didn't ask which one. He had four, and even though it was within the sanctions of the Qur'an, she still felt uncomfortable. She said she would ask Pir Baba to pray for Gafoor's wife and didn't take his money.

At eleven, Ashik and Asif arrived within minutes of each other. Minnie ignored Ashik. Asif walked in looking slightly more dyspeptic than last time, Sarah behind him in shalwar kameez with the dupatta over her head.

"Hi, Mom," said Sarah, kissing Minnie on both cheeks. "Saad and Samir send their love." They were Asif and Sarah's fraternal twins at college in Florida.

Taslima and Faruk came next.

And then, Cheryl showed up, with a crimson-faced, cried-out-eyed Naila next to her.

"Hello, Dadu," Minnie greeted her grandchild. Naila sniffled and broke down again, and Minnie took her in her arms.

The rest of the guests trickled in cutting it too close to the time of Pir Baba's arrival at noon, which didn't surprise Minnie because Bangladeshis were pitiful with time, and she maintained her jovial bearing welcoming them and, on a few occasions, dealing with their nosiness about how much the holy man was charging for his appearance at their house.

Minnie didn't let it affect her. She knew well enough how some of these people were, especially where money was involved, when gossip looked promising. Even above piety.

Good for Pir Baba for knowing his worth.

God wanted people to take care of themselves. He never said to roll around in squalor to show him devotion. He didn't ask for foolishness. There was a difference between greed and self-preservation, between selfishness and survival. There was a difference between empathy for suffering and destitution and grand shows of meekness and understanding of the plight of the poor. The real frauds were those latter types.

The guests settled in the living room with plates of food and drinks and tea. Because Minnie was not talking to anyone, no one knew how to behave. And because the air was thick with reverence, no one was intruding on its solemnity. Mustafa was trying his best to play host.

At noon, Minnie looked at the clock above the fireplace. It chimed. Bodies shifted with small relief, and using the cover of the hour's scales throats were cleared, coughs set free. They settled back in, their waiting resumed. A pair of eyes here and there tried to find another to meet. Minnie's attention didn't waver from the front door.

All those times Minnie shook her head and dismissed those End of Days believers for crackpots and crazies came back to her. What were they doing but waiting as she was now, with her houseful of believers—gossip and curiosity-seeking aside—for someone to bring them a sign. Yes, there were limits, and she had no inch to give to parents that killed their children in preparation for Judgement Day, they were not only crazy crackpots, they were sinners against the God they claimed to believe in, but the ones that waited, patiently, and it gave them hope, those who derided them were the sinners.

After a brief, hissed exchange between Ashik and Cheryl in the dining room, Ashik made his way to the front door, fidgety as a hound ready to spring. Asif was in the living room, faded to the background, his wife next to him holding his hand, which, as always, had him hemorrhoidal with discomfort. Cheryl was at the dining table, Naila next to her staring at the backyard out the window.

Ten minutes passed.

At twelve-twenty, Ashik looked at his mother and held up his hands.

Thirty minutes later, guests were asking to use the bathroom. A momentary dispersal took place, plates and teacups got refilled, and once more the party settled down, though not without a touch of impatience.

"So, where is he?" Ashik said. "Thank God you didn't pay in advance."

It was twelve-fifty exactly by the fireplace clock when the gravel in the driveway crunched under incoming tires.

Minnie opened the door and behind her the guests crowded the hallway to get a look.

"No wonder he charges extortion rates," Ashik hissed seeing the limousine.

Minnie walked out as the uniformed chauffeur came around and opened the back door.

As everyone was clearing the hallway and making room for Pir Baba's entrance, first one and then a second young woman climbed out of the limousine. They were Bangladeshi and looked like sisters. Behind Minnie, there was shuffling and darting of eyes.

The man could have relatives, Minnie thought. He was older now and needed more attention. Maybe they'd traveled with him from Bangladesh.

The girls offered their hands to the open door. Out of the air-conditioned dark of the limousine emerged a face Minnie had only imagined being real until then.

Pir Baba did not move in a hurry, and his gait was confident. He was a man used to being waited upon. He was not as tall as Minnie thought, and when Minnie greeted him, he took in her outstretched hand like an offered insult. Minnie mumbled an apology, mortified that she'd offended the holy man even before he'd taken a step inside her house.

"Please come in," Minnie said.

Pir Baba walked in and stopped just inside the door, the two girls at his elbows.

Minnie was suddenly afraid that there were too many people. The holy visit had been turned into an obscene show. A spectacle, a farce.

She wanted badly to say something, something worthy and humble to welcome Pir Baba, but anything she could think of fell short.

Pir Baba took a few more steps into the house. His eyes didn't make contact with anyone else's.

He fixed on a point straight ahead.

"Who is that?" he said, pointing past the guests. "That boy, who is that?"

Minnie closed her eyes, while everyone else tried to find who Pir Baba was pointing at.

"That boy," said Pir Baba. "He lives here?"

Minnie opened her eyes. Guests were looking from Pir Baba to her, but Minnie felt the presence of no one else other than Pir Baba, herself, and Ashraf.

"He did live here," Pir Baba answered himself. "He left." He didn't blink, and his stare was unnerving, but his expression soft, a mentor's or a loved one's, giving a sendoff. "Go now. It's fine, child. Go."

He closed his eyes and lowered his head. When he looked up again, he touched the tears on Minnie's cheeks with the back of his hand.

Minnie didn't move from where she was standing after Pir Baba left, and not even when her house cleared of guests. She said nothing to them, didn't respond to their goodbyes. Mustafa saw them out with Taslima's help, and when the house was down to just the family, Minnie was still standing at the door looking out at the empty driveway, the bag of money in her hands.

Seth Brady Tucker

Windmills

Archie awoke in a swirling fog, cool raindrops splashing on the soft leather of his wide-brimmed slouch hat, and if it weren't for the fiberglass vibrating beneath his shoulders, he would have thought he was dreaming about free-falling through dense clouds. His back hurt from napping against the sharp angles of the windmill's ceramic generator housing, and he could feel the bite of cold steel where his boots hung over the catwalk. His first waking thought was of Stephanie, and then of her stupid note, and even suspended above the earth like this he couldn't help but reach for her sleeping form next to him. She's gone, he thought, and no doubt.

The spring rain fell lazily around him, splattering quarter-sized spots on the narrow platform and his boots squeaked on the slick ceramic lacquer as he fumbled blindly for the ladder casement. A cold wind lifted the fog, and the Wyoming sky opened up blue and crystal all the way to the craggy spires of the Wind River Range, as if cut by a hatchet. Instead of vertigo, he felt a sensation of lonely peace as the world opened up. From one-hundred-fifty feet above the earth, the dirt ring where his old Chevy was parked looked cartoonish and symmetrically miniature and perfect.

No matter the weather, Archie never balked at the incredible heights at which he worked, never felt the unsteadiness that other mechanics complained about after work, their hands trembling as they drank banquet Coors from the can. He rarely even wore the climbing harness assembly or hard hats that were the required gear of all the mechanics for the gigantic Siemens machines, and last month, after climbing up the slick housing of a loose rotor without any safety gear, he was beginning to be known among the machinists by various nicknames like "Bounce" and "Pudding" and "Pulp," because the men who worked these new windmills knew what happened when someone lost respect for gravity, for the toll of flesh and bone owed the ground.

His disregard for the altitude also meant that he worked alone, no one willing to pair up with him unless it was strictly a two-person job. No one wanted to see firsthand what the dry and dusty soil of central Wyoming could do to the body, and not even the most sadistic roughneck workers wanted to be reminded of why no one else wanted to do these jobs. Fear was a part of it, but respect too. So he worked alone mostly, and instead of feeling lonely, Archie had simply gotten into the habit of taking naps in the afternoons, occasionally cracking some beers while he was fussing around in the innards of the machine, and after Stephanie left him, had even tried to read the books he had long ago promised her he would.

The wind picked up as Archie straddled the ladder welded to the white casing support, the stalled rotary blades began to spin again, their sound like a thump on an enormous cardboard box, then Archie was sixteen floors down in less than two minutes, one of the games he made up to stave off boredom. The beat of the blades was reassuring, each pulse like a heartbeat through his hands on the cold metal rungs, and even the sway of the whole unit made him sleepy again, like he was being rocked back and forth on the bosom of a gigantic robot mother. The other mechanics froze and locked the blades when they were working on the rigs, which to Archie was just about the stupidest waste of time imaginable. The other mechanics climbed up and down after each adjustment, starting and stopping the blades, tripling and quadrupling the time needed to make even small fixes to the windmills, and in Archie's opinion, the more times you crawled up the tower, the more dangerous the job became.

A big storm cloud was flexing its muscles over Elk Mountain and Beaver Rim, and the rain came down hard then as if poured from a bucket, then just as quickly turned to dry hail the size of rattlesnake eggs, and before Archie could get to his car he was drenched and stinging from the hard ice. Archie wouldn't be considered handsome by many women, but he had a dusty ruggedness that snared the occasional split-tail—he was tall, with thick ropy muscles running down his back and arms—and he still had his hair, which was better than most could say. Stephanie had hated his beer gut, and when Clark Blair, his best friend, discovered him doing sit-ups on the rig, he'd laughed and said, "Are you a fucking girl?" So, Archie worked out on his own time, or when no one was around.

He was busy combing his wet hair with his fingers when Clark pulled up in his rebuilt Mustang, and through the last efforts of the hailstorm, demonstrated his intent to head to the bar early by miming drinking down a huge beer and then another. Archie cranked his window down, a clot of hail peppering the inside of his car, and hollered, "Have the College Boys left yet?"

Clark couldn't hear him, leaned all the way across the bench seats and rolled the window down just a smidge. "What? Let's go drink beer at the Mule!"

"The College Boys," Archie yelled again, annoyed that Clark wouldn't roll his window down further so he could be heard, "have they left for the day?"

"The what? I said let's drink beer! Get in!" he yelled, mimed drinking again, and rolled the window back up as if everything had been decided.

Archie pulled his work shirt up over his head, pulled on a collared short-sleeve shirt that made him look like a bright green lollipop, wiped some fresh cow-shit off his boots, and climbed out of his car. It didn't matter where you were in Wyoming, there would be a camouflaged patty waiting. He dashed through the storm to the Mustang and as he made to get in, Clark acted like he was going to take off, which was just what Clark would do, no matter the situation. Archie suspected he would do this to his wife on their wedding day, if given the chance.

The Cunning Mule was old and dirty, hung like a warning just outside town, little more than a doublewide that had been bricked over with adobe stolen from the rubble of the old Shoshone tribal foundry. The *Mule* had no parking lot as it was two miles down an old dusty mining road, and cars simply parked anywhere there was space which made it look like a giant had simply tossed them there haphazardly like a handful of misshapen dice. Clark parked as far away from the other cars as possible. The hailstorm had diminished into a cold rain, just enough that they didn't need to run, but they both broke into a slow jog anyway; Archie to keep his hair straight, Clark to keep his shiny new silk "Mustang Mob" shirt from getting ruined. Archie had never seen Clark so excited by anything as he was about that car—most of the time, Clark was more concerned with things that "he just couldn't abide,"—so it was nice to see this new optimistic Clark flowering around the purchase of the vintage vehicle.

Two men wearing tan coveralls with steel-toed boots banged their way out the narrow door of the *Mule* in a bear-hug of camaraderie and made their way to a shiny new blue Dodge Charger, which Clark slowed to admire, and what he saw made the smile drain from his face. The paint job was fresh; a series of light blue flames pulsing from under the wheel-well of the vehicle and down the sides until it turned smoky and black at the trunk of the car. Archie recognized it as the exact replica of the orange flames searing down the side of Clark's Mustang, what the shop in Casper had guaranteed was a one-of-a-kind job. The only difference Archie could see was that where Clark's Mustang had his Airborne unit's motto, "Death From Above" stenciled in Latin on the hood, these men had "No Muff Too Tuff" in fat block letters. Clark stuffed his hands in his pockets as he walked past, staring sullenly at the men and the car, and said loudly, "What I can't abide, is these queers moving here from Timbuktu." The larger of the men, whether he had heard or not, flicked a cigarette butt into the stiff mud at their feet, where it hit Clark in his boot-heel, unnoticed, and Archie was able to corral him by the shoulders and steer him into the dark smoke of the bar with a promise of shots.

Inside, they recognized a few faces lining the bar but no sign of the new young bosses they called the college boys. The *Mule* had been a good place to drink when they were underage, empty mostly, but then Shoshone's population had tripled quickly over the last five years with the natural gas and energy company explosion, and suddenly there were jobs available for any dipshit country boy with nerves and no ethical problems concerning who and what they worked for. The murder and suicide rate had also spiked to six times what it had been when they were in high school, and it seemed like everyone was packing heat, especially the old ranchers around town, their disapproval of the changes to their town evident in the massive .40 caliber Colts they had strapped to their hips like nineteenth-century gunslingers.

Clark saw Stephanie first, her big hair and perfectly arranged scrunchie peeking from behind the last broad backs of the men at the bar. She had on a red and black flowered sleeveless dress with ruffles at the shoulders that showed off her muscular arms. Stephanie hadn't changed much since high school and the things she wore, the style of her hair, even her makeup, were almost entirely based on movies like *Sixteen Candles* and *Pretty Woman*. None of which was intended to be ironic.

Clark's mood had turned, and Archie tried to distract himself with a quick Depth Charge, even though his own heart was beating spastically, uselessly, in his chest from seeing her there. It had been but a few weeks since she left him, along with his engagement ring, on the Formica table in his half-kitchen, her note misspelled and straightforward and awful for it all, "I can't stay with someone whose gonta stay hear."

He'd known things weren't going well, that she wanted to leave Shoshone behind forever, leave everything she knew in the world simply because it was everything she knew in the world. Then, he'd landed the job with Siemens Energy, the job that had provided him with the money to buy the ring she always wanted, which it turns out was too little too late, and it wasn't lost on him that he'd taken the job in the first place to be able to marry Stephanie, and look at what that got him, which was losing Stephanie. So, he'd started drinking on the job a bit, started sleeping on top of the windmills, thinking over the mistakes he'd made, replaying the things that had led one to another to him losing her. He got to the part where he took the job so that he could finally ask her to marry him, then it jumbled into a confusing mess of action and inaction, the note, the ring, the fact that she even changed her cell number. Who does that with someone they've known for twenty years, he thought?

Clark pounded his beer, caught the shot in his teeth, circled his finger around the rim to the bartender for another, all without taking his eyes off Stephanie. "What I can't abide, is this Jezebel coming into what she must fucking *know* is our bar." Clark was nothing if not loyal, and in his mind, the treachery of Stephanie and the dishonesty of the owner of the detail and paint shop in Casper started to bleed into one another. The second round came, and he swallowed it back. "What I can't abide," he said, louder, "is the fact that bitch leaves you high and dry, and then is coming into our bar throwing it in our faces." Archie couldn't help noticing Clark was speaking about "their" relationship with Stephanie, so he steered Clark into the cracked vinyl seats of a booth where they couldn't see her anymore and ordered some rye whiskey for them both. The tabletop was a recycled and pitted oak door, with a brass nameplate reading "Saint John," a family that had dissolved and frittered away after one of their sons had gone missing in a coal mine. It was like that for most of the families who left the town—there was always a tragedy that precipitated the need for escape, to leave the poisonous nowhere that Shoshone so often became for successful families—before these same families disintegrated into shapeless masses of want and abandoned homes, spattered here and there all through Shoshone like old tractors rusting in a hayfield.

On the wall of the booth was mounted an old black and white photo of the first owner of the *Mule*, a thin-lipped balding man polishing an old fashioned glass with a dirty bar rag. Above the photo was a piano leg about the same length as a baseball bat, but thicker by half, lacquered and shiny, stained where the thinnest portion was used as the handgrip. Under the piano leg, spelled incorrectly in cracking black permanent marker, "Serbien Night Stick." Clark put his palm on the handgrip, sipped at his rye. “If it were that easy, right?”

“If what was that easy?” Archie asked, afraid to find out, the glimmer of mischievous boyishness normally behind Clark’s eyes replaced with a slack dullness, as if he was blinded by cataracts. It was the same look Clark had for the first year after he returned from Afghanistan.

“All-a this.” Clark answered, pointing to the whole bar. “Someone cheats you on a paint job, you take this and give em a whallop. Coupla queers come into town, copy your artwork? Give em a crack. Lying bitch whore comes slutting it up in your bar?”

“Now wait a minute Clark.”

“What wait a minute? Give em a crack right in their whore mouth. Teach em good that actions and words has consequences.” The bartender was already on his way with another round when Clark shook his glass at him, and when he arrived with the drinks, Clark asked him, “Who is Stephanie stepping out with tonight?” The bartender looked down the bar, shrugged, answered, “She come in alone. It’s ladies night. Not that you can tell, what with her being the only one. I should call it “lady” night.” The bartender smiled at his own joke, but no one laughed and he picked up the empties, wiped absently at the oak door. “That outfit look like it come from my high school prom date,” the bartender finished.

Archie felt like he still had to defend her honor, even with the note and all, “She says everything just fit better back then. It’s not like she doesn’t know it’s out of style. She dresses for comfort, which I suspect we can all totally respect.”

The bartender just shrugged and shuffled off, and Clark was watching Archie over the lip of his glass. “Now I get it. I see how it is.”

“What do you get?”

“You’re gonna try to get her back and then she’s gonna get you to move away and never come back.” The bar door swung open again and the two men with the Charger stumbled back in, followed by a cool draft of the smell of April rain on new concrete. They walked by the booth and the big one looked back as they cruised down the bar and took the seats on either side of Stephanie. Clark’s jaw set beneath his dark wispy beard. “It’s like I was saying,” he continued, “the problem with this country is that not enough of us get punched in the face for saying or doing something stupid. Someone says something, or does something, you got to worry what they got a gun, so you let it go. But just think about it—if you had to worry about getting your ass kicked for saying something asinine—I bet you’d think twice. Be a whole bunch of us watching what we said, being more careful with what we did."

Archie had to admit, it made some sense in a wild way, but asked, "So, you're saying we should all get our asses busted every time we say something stupid? That's like, censorship."

"How is that censorship? No one is stopping you from saying stupid things? And I'm not saying *all* the time. I'm just saying, the world would be a better place if at some point or another, we had all got our ass whupped for saying something stupid. Probably would take just the once. Like a consequence. The biggest problem with people these days is not enough of them have had their teeth kicked in for something they've said. It's about being proactive, really. Like a permanent 'caution' sign hanging behind the eyes so we watch what we say."

From down the bar, Archie heard a whoop and then the chatter of a couple of the regulars, and when he turned to look, he could see that the smaller man from the Charger was trying awkwardly to dance with Stephanie, bumping and fumbling his way to *Dire Straights*, "Money for Nothin," which issued from an ancient jukebox. She caught Archie's eye and widened them meaningfully, begging to be rescued, and it felt to him like a little apology. It was the first time she had acknowledged him since the split. He finished off his rye in one drink, straightened his hair, and made his way to where the man had her arched back in a dip. Her glorious titties were there behind the fabric of her dress for everyone to see, and instead of making him angry, it made him sad, because he had slept next to those breasts for over two years, every day but Wednesday when she worked the swing shift. "You mind if I cut in?" he asked, reaching for her wrist.

"The fuck you are," said the little man, as he pulled her away in a graceful ballroom move.

"Listen," Archie said, about to issue an ultimatum he had thought out on his way down the bar, but too late, as he saw Clark streak past him, leg up, his cleated boot connecting with the man's chest, sending him crashing into the old pinball machine in the corner. Clark stood over the man, said, "Watch your mouth, Dodge."

The larger of the two was so stunned that he tried to finish drinking the beer he had pressed to his lips, spilling a bit down his goatee and into his coveralls. Clark held his hand up, and said, "Gather your friend and let's take it outside. No need to ruin everyone's night." The man stopped as if thinking about the reasonableness of this offer, hauled his friend up by the lapels, replied, "You done fucked up, Porkchop."

"Your name's Porkchop," Clark replied, which made Archie want to laugh and just stop the whole thing. It was high school all over again. He was still holding Stephanie's wrist, realized there was no need and let it drop. "I guess we're going outside now," he apologized, and pulled a barstool out for her, and she said sadly, "Clark aughtn'ta jumped in so quick. You'd-a handled it," and he knew that he was right back in it, for good. She took the two shots the men had ordered and downed them, then followed.

Outside, Clark started warming up, dancing on his toes, throwing crazy looking hay-makers, dodging, dipping, lurching back and forth, stretching his legs, shaking his head back and forth as if he were clearing the cobwebs. He looked ridiculous. But anyone who knew Clark's reputation would be getting the hell out of there, would know that he was made from an iron forged in the fires of Army boxing smokers and Tough Man contests, that the military tattoos running crisscross over his body were not only for show. Clark was a warrior—fearless and willing to descend into the dark pit of violence in ways that seemed innate to him—it had been like that on the battlefield, it was said, but he never spoke of it even when Archie had found a box of medals under his couch. The other two men were staring at him, their hands on their knees, smiling at one another, like they couldn't believe what they were seeing, looking from one another to the spectacle of Clark getting ready to whoop ass. It was too bad for them, Archie thought, because there was no doubt what was coming. Only the smaller man seemed even remotely as concerned as they should have been, his fat hands going up to finger nervously at the footprint indentation on his chest.

Archie knew it would do no good, but he tried to talk Clark out of it anyway. Clark was in what he called "full gorilla burn," and wasn't having it. His smile was wide and insane looking, and he finished the depth-charge he had carried out with him, then took Archie's beer from him and drank that. Finished, he calmly walked across the dirt parking lot to where the two men sat waiting on their Charger, arms crossed, expecting an argument before things ramped up. The big one didn't even have time to put his hands up. His smile shattered in an explosion of fist and lips and he disappeared over the other side of the car in a heap.

The little one tried to run.

Clark chopped down on both collar-bones, punched him in the neck, twirled him around and sent him sprawling with a tremendous kick to the ass. The man stayed down, like they always did when Clark's rage came calling. Not a word had been said, which is how Clark liked it. Put up or shut up, he liked to say. He strode up to Archie, took a cigarette from his pocket, lit it. As if in explanation, he said, "You got to hit em hard the first time. Take the piss out of them." He took another long thoughtful drag, "Guess I better git," he said.

Stephanie had watched from the doorway, and now she walked around Clark suspiciously and put her hand lovingly on Archie's arm, spoke only to Clark, "You're too drunk to drive, you get another Dewey they send you up again." She looked at the men, then back, "Jeez you didn't have to try to kill them," then to Archie, "He's too drunk to drive Arch. You seen him stumble what with the last one. He ain't driving you home."

Clark ran his hands through his hair, leaving a pink steak at the temple, pulled what looked like a tooth out of his knuckle. "Yeah," he sighed. "I guess you two is getting back together then." He seemed saddened by the thought, his hands falling to his side in forfeit. "I'll just go sleep it off in the 'Stang." He tossed Archie the keys. "Just put em up under the wheel so they can't take me in for having em in the ignition." He stretched his back, looked at the darkened sky, "These fuckin assclowns always start it up on the nicest nights, don't they?" He absently picked at a piece of flesh on his knuckle. "Cops come, tell em I split? They won't know the new car anyhow." Clark moved off toward his vehicle like a child in bootied pajamas, scratching at his backside like he'd been sentenced to bed too early. In another world, he would have been heroic, his devotion and love for his friend the tragic flaw novels were written about. But Clark had come back from his war mean in a way that would only seem noble to his closest friends—mean in a way that had changed from someone good in a fight before he left—to someone dangerous and wild when he returned. It was something they didn't talk about, and even for their closeness, Archie still didn't know what Clark had done over there—the only thing Clark ever talked about was how bad the food was—how cold the desert mountains could be.

Archie and Stephanie waited by the door to the *Mule*, watched a couple other men gather up the two unfortunate fighters and help them stumble back to the restrooms in the back. When they were sure the cops were not coming, Stephanie took Archie's hand in hers and walked over to the new Mustang. Clark was already dead asleep, boots up on the dash, head lolled back and mouth open and drooling. "He ain't never liked me," Stephanie said, as if she just realized it.

"No," Archie replied, "I think he just loves me too much, is the problem." He laid the keys on top of the driver's side tire, "He'd give up all he has, fight off an army, for me. And he don't even know I ain't worth-a-half of it, and probably couldn't do the same for him." Archie rubbed some dust off the fender of the car with his forearm. "You got to believe, to be like him." He thought about smoothing Clark's hair, thought better of it. "It woulda been better for him if he'd-a just stayed in the Army, found a better life somewhere out there. But all he could think about over there was coming back home. To all this nothing."

Stephanie put her hand on Archie's beltline, let it linger and fall. "You want to come back to my apartment with me, Arch?"

"I got a better idea," he said, brightening. "You ever been up on a Siemens WP Cyclops? Biggest windmill in the world. The new one even has an elevator on the side."

The drive to the new windmill was a short one, and even with the steering wheel in her hand she managed to fish around in his pants for his penis, stroking it absently. It was the way she had always been, and it was this fearlessness that he loved most about her. Her car was filled with fast food bags and half empty wax cups bulging weakly in their holders. They made out as the elevator climbed, and Archie had to stop her from going down on him because he knew he'd have nothing left for the top if she did. When the elevator cage rattled to the stop, he walked her out to the safety railing, where they could see Shoshone idling ten miles to the west, then the burnt shape of what was Medina, a town that had literally burned to the ground a decade earlier, to the east. Archie was drunker than he expected, the booze burning in his empty gut, and could feel the tug of the abyss as they leaned against the railing kissing as if they were starved for one another. The blades were turning slowly in the cold wind, which was at least fifteen degrees cooler than it had been down at ground level. Stephanie took his hand and jammed it up under her top, and when he put his other hand up her dress, he could feel the lace panties for a moment before she pulled them aside for him so he could more easily get to her. It was this audacity that always kept him coming back. She bore down on his hand as he kissed her, their tongues mining what felt like foreign country, and she quickly pushed him against the railing and straddled her heels pulling him deeper.

The breeze powering the blades pulsed with every movement she made, and the railing in his hands was cold enough to send chills up and down his spine, the bolts creaking as she bore down hard on him, and he came as hot and heavy as he ever had in his life. She slowed the cadence of her strokes as if she was finished, then slowly picked the pace up again, her hands free and heels barely hooked into his buttocks, one slip away from a terrible plunge. She came again, something so unusual and wonderful, something he loved too, goose bumps roughening her thighs and her arms. He was surprised to find that he could probably keep going, the danger of the fall somehow turned erotic.

They slumped down onto the metal and ceramic housing, and Archie sat behind her with their legs out between the railing and over the sides of the windmill, two hundred feet between the soles of their shoes and the patched dirt. Archie thought he should say something, cement their relationship again, beg her to move back in so they could return to the way things were, and he knew that was exactly what she wouldn't want, so he remained silent. To the east, he could see headlights from one of the gigantic loaders speeding up a dirt road on the way to the highway that ran parallel to the wind farm, and from the immense height and distance, it was like watching a lumbering scorpion crawl its way across a concrete sidewalk.

He watched the white clouds of the dust fan out in the darkness behind the rig, his head on Stephanie's shoulder. She pointed at the highway to the west. "Someone's coming," and it was like Archie knew what would happen before it happened, and he knew that the car speeding from the west was surely Clark's, and the inevitability of everything that had ever happened in the world suddenly seemed sure to lead the Mustang into the welcoming lights of the rig, and Archie froze with this prescience, and the ramifications of his decision to choose Stephanie over Clark became palpable, how for all his living days he would grapple with a future already set; a destiny fixed by the one frozen expression of his weakness for this woman. They watched, mesmerized, as the car and truck closed with one another, the vehicle rising the slow incline, invisible twilight behind the massive truck—over the rise together, the great white fist hitting flat into the smaller knuckles of a dark fist, and even though it had seemed preordained to Archie—the physics of the accident left him shaking as they rose to their feet and ran to the elevator.

When they reached the accident, both out of breath, Archie could see that the tan coal-truck's bumper was bashed in, but otherwise undamaged, and the driver was sitting on the dusty upslope of the shoulder of the road, head in his hands. Clark's Mustang looked strange, oddly colored, was bent upwards in the middle like an inchworm frozen mid-crawl, and there was a dark patch of oil pooling under the wreck.

Clark's arm was dangling leisurely from the driver's side of the car, and Archie slid down onto the asphalt between the crumpled vehicle, only then seeing that it was the Charger, and took Clark's hand in his. He couldn't summon the courage to look into the interior of the vehicle, afraid of what he would see. The engine began to tick as the heat dispelled. Clark groaned and was confused, his eyes tracking but not registering anything until suddenly a big crazy grin came over his face, blood on his teeth, "Them boys ain't gone never figure out how they car got here in this fix."

"What did you do, Clark? What is all this?" he said, not sure he wanted the answer.

Across the road, Stephanie was talking calmly with the driver of the truck, alternating between him and her cellphone, and Archie could suddenly see what his future life would look like without Clark's misguided advice to aid him and it was his first true experience with that hot electric fear running along his spine—the little house he would buy and fix up, Stephanie happy until the wedding and all the fun was over, their jobs slowly pulling them apart like saltwater taffy—then the affairs and the late nights with him waiting for Steph to come home from the bars. Their children. Spoiled and made fools by a mother's coddling, his ascent of the windmills increasing with the new responsibilities and the effort to satisfy her many needs, more carelessness. And Clark would disappear, an empty space in the world they inhabited like the blemished silver in an old rearview mirror, their resentment of each other increasing at the same rate as the thumping windmill blades spinning up in a storm; the sound of failure like a weak heartbeat pulsing on and on for no good reason at all.

He stroked Clark's rough hands, the faint red imprint from his tangle with the two men stark against the white of his knuckles. Clark began to laugh at whatever joke it was he had played on the men. Archie stood up and without asking took a heavy box of tools off the loader and set to freeing Clark from the vehicle, wrenching with all of his strength on a crowbar as Clark's laughter brought tears to his eyes, the door squealing as if it refused to give up his friend until it did.

His plan was to leave Stephanie to her car, get a ride back into town on the loader maybe, pick up the Mustang and take his friend home. He would ask Clark what it all meant, maybe even what it was from his war that allowed him to love and to hate like this, how they had all arrived here at this terrible moment. Archie pulled off his shirt and held it to a deep wound along his friend's sternum, confident that Clark would know what to do once the blood from all his injuries was finally washed away.

Tony O'Keeffe

At the Concert

A month before the concert, a strange thing occurred. A deep melancholy took possession of me. A feeling I had never known before. I have been happy in my marriage of twenty-four years. I work for an important company, and am respected and, I think, liked by my colleagues. I have long been content.

On the night of the concert, my wife and I had to park several blocks away from the performance hall. (There was a rare full house, because one of the great cellists was scheduled to perform.) We walked through a cold drizzle, hand in hand, making light of the chill, a small inconvenience in light of the pleasure to come.

The first portion of the performance was pleasant—familiar music well played. But there was a disturbance, in the middle of it. I heard some sounds of distress, perhaps ten or fifteen rows behind us. When I turned to look, I could see that an elderly woman had fallen into some kind of difficulty. The ushers were with her, and soon a small group of emergency workers arrived, and carried her away. The orchestra had continued to play during all of this, which I imagine they had long been trained to do.

When the intermission came, my wife chose to remain in her seat, as I knew she would; she very much dislikes the commotion of the crowd and especially its generally empty chatter about the performance. But I went to the lobby eagerly. My new young lover was going to meet me there. She is a photographer and wanted to take a picture of me in my silly tuxedo. I worried about how to find her. But she had chosen to stand on a stairway, just a few steps above the crowd. And she stood like a quiet island amid all the bustle, easy to find. When I first saw her, I had the strangest desire. I wished that, for a minute or two, she had become completely naked, revealed to all those people milling about with their drinks and chat. I wanted them to know how beautiful she was, and how proud I was to have proved worthy of her love, of her desire for me.

I brought a glass of cheap "champagne" to her and posed for my picture. We did not spend more than a minute together, and even that felt dangerously indiscreet.

The second half of the evening was dominated by the performance of the genius. It swept me away from everything but the desire to see my lover naked once more. There was much applause, much joy for all of us who were privileged to hear such rare, lovely music.

When my wife and I left the auditorium, we crossed the street to begin walking back to our car (the night had become even colder, the rain heavier). Across that street there was a crowded bus stop. When I looked at it, I saw her, small and vulnerable to the cold. My concern for her passed through me like a moment of pain. And I wondered how much time would pass before I betrayed her too.

Erik Peters

Blame

"I'm going to ask you again. Did you take Eva's Christmas chocolate?"

"No! I already told you!"

"Well, the evidence is pretty convincing, young man.

"No, it isn't! You're lying!"

"You ate all your chocolate in one week. Since then, you've been pestering your sister for hers. Now suddenly there's no chocolate in her stocking and the only one upstairs was you." She was counting on her fingers. That meant she was angry. "Can you explain all that?"

I sulked for a minute. "I didn't do it! She's just a big stupid liar!"

"Erik! Go to our room this instant! When you're ready to fess up and apologize you can come back down!"

"Fine!" I shrieked. I turned and stomped up the stairs, slamming my bedroom door behind me. I could hear Eva wailing and mum trying to soothe her.

I was not usually a temperamental child, but I hated—and still hate—being blamed for things I didn't do. When I am accused of something unfairly, I lose my mind. Even as an adult it is one of the few things that makes me fly right off the handle.

Maybe that's why I've always loved animals. We had dogs when I was growing up, but my closest companions were always my pet rats. No matter how sad or angry or generally upset I was, the rats were always there, peering at me with their shiny, innocent eyes.

Despite their fearsome reputations, rats are extremely social and bright. Watching them play together is still something I enjoy. They may steal food from one another, scrap, and even pee on your arm to 'claim' you, but there is something special about their animalian innocence, their purity so absent in people, how they groom one another, miss dead companions, and sleep in a pile. Their immediacy, which knows no future and no past, has always calmed me.

When I had slammed my door, I stomped across the room, trying desperately to let them hear me downstairs and then threw myself down beside the bed. Tears welled up in my eyes and I scrunched myself up into as tiny a ball as I could.

As my vision cleared, the rat cage, which sat directly across from me, came slowly into focus. Ivory, my beautiful she-rat, was there, staring through the bars. Her sisters must have been sleeping in their lightbulb box house.

Ivory was a particularly intelligent rat, able to outsmart any latch or lock. At first, we had tried everything to keep her in the cage my father had built, but it was to no avail. Eventually we gave up and everyone watched where they stepped when they were upstairs.

I reached forward, lifted the latch, and pulled her out, cradling her in my arms. She stood up on her hind paws and began licking the tears from my cheeks. It was such a sweet gesture from so blameless a creature that it made me shake with sobs all the more.

Why couldn't they see I was innocent? I would never have taken Eva's chocolate. I was a bit of a glutton, perhaps, but never dishonest or thieving. Stupid Eva must have eaten all her chocolate and blamed me. But I knew in my heart that that was not true . . . she never did that kind of thing.

Ivory stopped licking my cheeks and settled into the crook of my arm. It was the middle of the day, so she had no interest in her nocturnal escapades. I looked down at her sleek milk-and-coffee fur. Why couldn't I be like that? She never had to worry about getting into trouble. She never had to worry about doing the wrong thing. About being blamed! Heck, a rat *can't* do the wrong thing, even a 9-year-old knows that! She had no conscience. She lived right now, and only right now. She did what she wanted and was always innocent, even when she caused harm. Why couldn't I be like that?

I was so angry I began to cry again. My convulsing chest must have roused Ivory because she looked up, sneezed, and started cleaning her face. After a moment, she jumped off my arm and darted under the bed. I rolled onto my side to watch her.

As my eyes adjusted to the dusty dimness I gasped. There was all Eva's Christmas chocolate. Ivory flitted nimbly between half-opened wrappers, nibbling here and there as she went.

I stared aghast for a moment. This cleared me entirely. All I had to do was go downstairs and tell mum. She would *have* to apologize to me. So would Eva! That would be so sweet I could almost taste it! I raised myself on one elbow and nearly got up.

I paused, then lowered myself again and stared into the gloomy, chocolate strewn space under my bed. Without thinking, I reached forward and in one sweeping movement brought all the chocolate, one very startled she-rat, and a great number of dust bunnies out into the center of the room.

I sat there for some time, chalk-white lines still staining my cheeks, gorging on as much Christmas chocolate as I could cram in my mouth. Ivory grabbed one or two pieces and replaced them under the bed (this time out of my reach).

The two of us sat contentedly, eating. We had both been innocent when I came into the room. But now only one of us was. And guilt tasted great.

Kelly Craig

WE COOK A FAMILY MEAL

We cook a family meal while the man upstairs is dying slowly. We chop onions, carrots, celery. We fry them in butter. We try to teach the children underfoot that this is called *mirepoix.* They reach a playful din and are scolded by one of the other death watchers. The dog eats a stray carrot dice from the floor.

Before dinner we wash our hands furiously. We speak of contagion, of how long you must stand next to an infected person before you too become infected. We make plans to work from home, to work from this home, the home of the man who is upstairs dying. The toddler trips over the oxygen cannula running across the carpet.

We go to the grocery store to buy food for everyone waiting in the house with the man who is dying. We buy Goldfish crackers for the children. We scan the shelves for the dying man's favorite flavor of applesauce, but the store is empty of such long-lived pantry staples. We buy the last four pots of another flavor. It is the only food the dying many can eat. Shoppers wear gloves. We avoid touching our faces. We don't know about masks yet. I stand protectively over the cart while you dash for the last cardboard palette of canned tomatoes. We wait in line near the milk refrigerator. We wait an hour. We wash our hands.

The man dying slowly upstairs hears about the contagion from the snippets of our conversation, from the divulgences of his bedside visitors, from the news on the radio that plays his favorite classic rock in his room. He has been dying much longer than the rest of us, dying of a contagion originated and propagated within him. He reminds us that our bodies can kill us without any help from other organisms. We make a family dinner. We say a toast to the man who is dying upstairs, as if he is different from all of us.

The man dying slowly upstairs dies more quickly than we expect. He leaves us behind in the chaotic world to miss him with nowhere to go. We go to the grocery store and buy the last can of pinto beans on the shelf. We stay inside. We wash our hands. We get stoned. We make love, unexpectedly, surprised that we have anything of ourselves to give to each other. We make no plans to formally remember the man who died, and we remember him only privately. His death makes us want to do what you are supposed to do when someone dies, *go on*, but we sit, stuck, the world in an ominous pause, shimmering after spring rain, unable to go anywhere.

The spring is cruel. It leaves us out, to rebirth ourselves. We try to redeem this time. We bake bread. We do pushups. We make lists of all the things we need to clean. We go on long walks to feel the relief of the sun and the blossoms. But the moment we are grieving is unredeemable, and we are stuck in it.

We sit on the back patio and drink wine and watch a rat root around in the garden patch, yet uncultivated, covered over with winter's dead. The rat is one of the many creatures who has come to take back the neighborhood now that humans are staying indoors, cars left unstarted to scare them away. We see new neighborhood cats, baby squirrels, quail families. We hear stories of deer coming down from the foothills and coyotes wandering up from the desert. Stuck in the middle of town, nothing quite so wild reaches us.

Summer ushers in deadly stillness. The rat in the garden patch gathers sticks and leaves and carries them back to the neighbor's abandoned shed where he makes his home. His rat nest in a rat nest year in a rat nest world. Unburdened, he hops cutely across the yard. Carrying his load, he scampers, almost slithers through the grass. *Rat, in the garden patch. Rat, sliding through the grass.* Drunk, we describe his movements in singsong, exhilarated by the dynamism of his rat life.

The first breath of fall takes our breath away. A windstorm shakes the city awake and out, into a new season. It takes down ancient trees and powerlines. It has us looking back to times when we walked under trees that now sit in bits in a pile like so much trash. Looking back to times we talked to each other in their shade, sharing the intimate words that you can only share in the anonymity of the outdoors, where they float away without getting trapped in the corners of rooms. Our lives are stripped down while we wait for outside forces to restore our power. We read and write and eat cold, simple food by candlelight. We sit in each other's company and bask in our gentle way of holding each other up. I sit alone, in silence.

These days I am afraid for the future of everything. My journal includes lists of supplies I'll need in various types of emergencies: in the event where I still have utilities but it is unsafe to leave my house; in the event that I am stuck in my house without utilities; in the event that I leave in my car; in the event that I run out of the house with only a backpack. I write down where I might run to. I advise myself to take the car, if possible.

I watch the wind push around dirty air against a cloudless sky and I put my hand on top of the coffee pot while it brews to see if it will burn me. I cry one breathless, panicked cry in the aisle of the garden store because a woman who looks like me isn't wearing a mask. When confronted, she has no answer to my question, when an answer is all I am looking for.

An old friend writes to me that she is having trouble keeping up with her work because the virus has caused her heart to swell. Doctors don't know why or how to stop it. I want her and her swelling heart to walk with me in the garden center and confront the maskless woman.

I try wearing a barrette in my hair to add excitement and variety to my life. It makes me look like a child, and when I try to remove it, I realize I have mislaid the clasp and it is stuck in my hair; I am stuck as a child. My heart swells when later I sit down in your office chair and you remove it gently. The barrette is dead in my hand, and I am an adult once again.

Before any of it is over, I attempt to eulogize the man who died upstairs. I talk about his love of the movie *The Shawshank Redemption*. I liken these months we've spent alone in separate houses without him to serving a sentence for a crime we did not commit. I learn from others who kept watch over the man as he died that he always kept mushroom gravy in the house, just for me, a vegetarian. I attempt to eulogize him, but I come up short, stuck on the mushroom gravy, every day the same as the day that he died.

We cook a family meal. This time, we cook inside alone, while the family waits on the patio in seats far away from each other, faces covered. They enter the house to serve themselves one by one. We play soccer on the lawn with the children. We sit six feet away from them in the grass and teach them to fold origami flowers. The children remind us that we are in a springtime of our lives. We are crocuses. We are hunkering down in the nourishing soil to blossom when we are allowed to blossom again.

Neema Muneer

The Price One Pays

It has been three days since our home plunged into silence, since anyone has spoken in this household. The quiet, though welcome at first, is fast outgrowing the relief and is letting in a very heavy air of uneasiness, but only for me, it seems. The youngest of our lot is just five years old and even she does not look tempted to tear open the dark veil that has descended upon us. Effortlessly, everyone seems to be floating from screen to platter to couch, sometimes even to the floor, like the characters in some mute play, and has not yet let out any audible need for each other or for anything; completely preoccupied with themselves and whatever it is that swims in their heads and minds. I am definitely beginning to worry and feel more than a bit lost, a certain fear gnawing at my nerves.

It was I who had raised a finger at the dinner table in a new attempt to bring down the regular din and the raised voices. I had solemnly declared that I would not tolerate another sound or syllable from any of them, that indeed if they dared to pay no heed to that warning of mine, I would simply pluck out their tongues and sever their heads off. Yes, I do realize now that perhaps I should not have been that harsh. That was about seventy hours ago, and I haven't heard a sound since from any of them, not a breath. Somehow, every other source of noise that I was accustomed to also seems to have dissipated. In the morning today, I noticed that the birds had come to perch on the railing of the balcony, but I did not hear them exchange pleasantries as usual or rant about their surroundings. Even the way they clucked at the seeds I had left for them was done in utmost silence. I quietly crept behind the curtains to spy on them but no, I was right, everything was eerily quiet.

My ego forbade me from telling the kids directly to quit their act. Instead, I stealthily put their devices on high volume, hoping that would break the ice when they turned to it. But amazingly, when all three sat down with their screens, like programmed automatons, not a bleep could be heard. I wondered if the game had gone too far and negotiated with myself—should I simply ask them to speak or just roughly tickle them back to themselves? But I could not prompt myself to do it. Not only had they stopped speaking aloud, it was almost as if they could not see me either. Even though my daughter looked up at me each time

I passed her by, I felt something had glazed over her eyes and she was not exactly looking at me. As for my son, I had stopped making such emotional deductions about him long ago, for stepping into adolescence had surely played a trick on him. The distance between us was now at least a few years old. His mother had simply become someone he had started to sidestep, someone he could work with if he played carefully. A hindrance he had progressively learnt to navigate, and this from that kid who would not sleep a full night without my arms around him.

I sat myself down and picked up a paperback. Surely, I was stressing over nothing. I tried to encourage myself to enjoy the temporary bliss, to just sit and read the goddamned book without having to put it down for someone else, wasn't this what I had wanted for a very long time now? How many years has it been that the canals of my ears had been clogged with unnecessary noise? The incessant crying of infants through a whole decade, one after the other, through long nights and agonizing days, then their adamant scowls and tantrums as toddlers and the cunning ploys of my feebly mustachioed teenager; ugh, truly it had all been too much. Always sound slapping me about; while I ate, slept, thought, read, wrote; why even when I fucked, always cut short or made quicker. And what about the nasal speech of the man I lived with? What kind of love had I harbored for him that for all these years I had not screamed in pure agony as I lived with that voice of his in the background, day after day, month after month, year after year? Then, there was the Mothership herself, always a whine away from complaint, the biggest baby of them all, even at sixty! Her sound could instantly bake up fresh batches of guilt in me every time I so much as looked at her. It was always I, the bitch of a daughter or Them, the bastard of a world that seemed to leave her distressed. Her aggrieved sound would needle into me mid-slumber even. And then the sound of devices, machines, vehicles, other mortals, and all the sounds that emanated from nature itself . . . how had I put up with it all for so long?

I know how—I had tried to survive the years by acting like I was listening, by always saying *Yes*. I had reheated a thousand cups of tea over and over again, for close to twenty years now, never having the chance to gulp it down in one stretch, always interrupted, always having to put that cup down and go wherever the hell the call for help summoned me. I had allowed noise to permeate the very fiber of my being, stretching me here and there, through irregular resentful corners, slowly filling me up over the years like an incongruous, distorted balloon, asking me to always present myself, to assist, to be at the world's beck and call, reassuring myself foolishly that someday things would quieten down, that words of appreciation and periods of respite would find their way to me, knowing fully well that would be only when I'd land on my death bed, or maybe not even then. Over the years, there had been nothing left of me for myself, some sound or the other had always hollered and my conditioned mind had carried my limbs over to it, ready for service. I had suppressed every cry for help that had risen in my own chest, shushing it mercilessly, always commanding myself to keep waiting. I had run towards everyone and everything but never towards myself. Just a mere review of the noise I had put up with prompted me to push the book away and lulled me into an exhausted slumber.

When I woke up, I saw my mother in the kitchen, a rare sighting. I slowly walked up to her and she turned to me, a cup of freshly brewed tea in her hands. She handed the cup to me with a smile and walked away. As unbelievable as it seemed to be, I knew it was mine and took a sip. A feeling of utter bliss cruised through me and I followed my mother to the dining room where she took the first seat and I took the one opposite to hers. I thought she would make an attempt to lure me into conversation, but she had already picked up the newspaper and started scanning it with utmost concentration. The doorbell rang then, and my son walked towards it, but not a footstep was heard. He opened the door to his father who shuffled in, loaded with bags of groceries. My son took a few from him and together they walked to the kitchen and started to sort the bags out, silently. Worry began to worm its way through my skin. I did not have it in me to ask my husband if I may get him his evening tea, something told me it would not be needed anymore, as it had not been the past two days. And indeed, he got down to it himself just after he changed into his home clothes. I wondered how long this state would last and what I was supposed to do if it did. I tried thinking back to how I had spent the last two days, what exactly had I filled my hours with, now that the world was in no dire need of my services? My hands began to sweat as I realized I had no recollection whatsoever of what had happened in the hours that had already passed since my world had gone mute. When I saw my husband meekly walk to the bedroom with his cup in hand, I followed him inside.

"Sheffin, look at me!" I reached out for his empty hand just as we got in the room, almost together. He calmly placed his cup on the dresser and turned around to look at me. My eyes brimmed over when he continued to simply look into me, but would not utter a word. He did not even ask me why I had called him. I rubbed my forehead on his chest and the tears began to flow. A part of his shirt started to soak but his arms did not rise to hold me. After a minute, I looked up at him and implored, "Sheffin, say something! Please!" He stepped back then and walked towards his computer and sat down on the chair. His tea lay ignored and grew cold.

For a few slow hours, I sat staring at the solitude that for years I had prayed so hard for. I could only sit and watch as one child of mine washed herself and then another served and fed himself. Later, my mother was seen holding hands with my husband, a perfect camaraderie between them, as they sat down in front of the television, now rendered mute as well but still functioning otherwise. The next day, my fourth day into this tragedy, a peep into the balcony showed that the hibiscus plant had grown new leaves overnight, regaining her luster, and for the first time the roses too had flowered. I was sure I hadn't watered them in days and the transformation that came over them was as if a whole season had changed. I looked down at the floors, closely, with narrowed eyes, to see if they needed a swipe with the broom, but nowhere could I find my fallen strands of hair in the usual corners, always the foremost reason the apartment would beg for a brooming. I looked into the school mail to see if the teachers had written, after all none of us had gone near any homework, but no, not a single line from even them. Finally, in a bid to initiate contact, I grabbed a comb from the kids' room and walked towards the youngest child; she always needed help with her tangles. As I neared her, she quietly took the comb from me and started to find her way through her mane. I could sense the beginning of another choke as I saw her little fingers learn quickly, so I moved away, looking down, unable to look for another face to cling to. I felt like a lone traveler in space, fallen too far from actual life, our tiny apartment now a galaxy of cancelled noise; acknowledging that our once bustling cocoon had started to close in on me, and my chest could only tighten up in response.

Vicki Derderian

Veil

In this house, my grandmother's house, the smell of perspiration and melted butter. In this house, percolating coffee hiccups arrhythmically and my grandmother uses a sawed-off broomstick to roll filo dough as white and satiny as a wedding dress.

A tear in the dough. A batch thrown out.

Her right wrist, jangles with charms, silver silhouettes of her grandchildren. Though the charms are identical, we are not. My cousins have gold woven in their hair, green eyes, noses that are pugs, buttons. I am a dark brown girl with black frizz hair. My grandmother prefers my cousins—pretty children of her son, number one son, my uncle who she dotes on. My mother is not her favorite. Who doesn't want to be their mother's favorite?

In this house, my grandmother's house, coffee and baklava, bitter and sweet. Cups and saucers clatter and spoons stir sugar. Sips and hums. My mother slumps at the table, aggrieved. She has left another job, told never to set foot again, things have been going badly for her and she needs help. The worst kind of help. Help from her family.

"They hate me, you know." She insists. "They really do."

When you are ten years old, you don't question any of this. You listen. You listen to your mother when she tells you she doesn't need anyone's help. You believe her when she says she is tough, resilient. You don't wonder if your mother is reliable or not. Of course, she is reliable.

In this house, my grandmother's house, my cousins pull Taki's tail, the cat yowls. "My turn your turn, no, my turn my my my my." Hide and Seek with no rules. "*Meg yergoo yarreck.*" One, two, three.

"Go." My mother tells me. "Go play."

I am not going anywhere. Is love the tether? Is fear?

I crawl under the big mahogany table where my family's feet and legs line the perimeter: flesh-colored stockings and terry scuffs, my grandmother. Brown loafers, one with a penny, one missing, my uncle. Smooth meaty calves and worn black pumps, my mother. I nest under her chair holding onto a claw foot, arched like Taki, wanting to purr.

"Anahid," my uncle speaks in Armenian, beginning every sentence with my mother's name. Anahid. Anahid. Anahid.

In this house: a language of secrets.

Her foot bounces up and down, up and down. I will not topple. I will not make a sound. Anahid. Anahid. Anahid.

"*Esheg.*" My mother cries out. Asshole. A curse.

I feel a sharp kick hit my soft belly. And another and another. Three blind kicks,

But I stay where I am.

She finds me under the table. "Go." My mother wails. "Now."

She locks me in a room that reeks of stale face powder, my grandmother's bosom. In this room, a narrow iron bed covered in crochet that I will sleep in that night and every other night for the next eight years.

After I read my poem, there's stunned silence and respectful, if tepid applause, but I'm triumphant. At the New Student Reception, flushed from too much free wine, I forgo the cheese cubes, the pyramid of stale crackers, the bear hugs and air kisses, and march myself over to the table of an important writer, one whose notice I crave. At twenty-seven, I'm one of the older students in the program and she, a visiting professor, is only a few years older than me.

"Lovely. A lovely poem." The important writer says, "And you were raised by her, by your grandmother, right?"

I want to tell the important writer everything. How I write and write and write because my life depends on it. How my history is everything because I need something beyond myself because myself is not good enough, because I am nothing.

"She was born in the village of Marash around 1900." I respond eagerly in a voice that sounds reedy and high, compared to her assured baritone. "There is no exact date, no birth certificate, no one left who knows. There was no mention of her father who was probably rounded up, or something so horrific that it cannot take the form of words. It is an incomplete picture."

"Armenians? Ah. Yes. The Genocide."

"Yes, so when she was fifteen? Before escaping to Aleppo, her mother left her in an orphanage. When she was sixteen? When she was seventeen? Amoo plucked her out of the orphanage, selecting her as a bride for his brother back in America."

"Plucked from the orphanage?" The writer's magnificent halo of blonde curls spring up and down with each nod. "Amazing!"

I bask in her attention. “Yes. She and Amoo sailed to Marseilles. There’s this great photo of her there . . .”

The old snapshot: round chin and shining eyes, her flowered babushka and jaunty Breton striped shirt.

“The photo in your poem?”

“No, no, another one. Completely different. They stayed there for several weeks, months, a year maybe and she married by proxy.”

“By proxy? Can you imagine?” Another first-year student has squeezed in next to her and she glances over to her for assent. “The fortitude? What she has endured?”

“When she finally made it to America and married this man she never met, well, my grandpa, she had in quick succession two children, girl, boy. But the boy, the son was what mattered.”

“Uh huh,” says the important writer, who is not incidentally, a brilliant woman. “Of course, he was. Tell me, do you speak the language?”

I shrug. “Some curse words . . .”

“This is so interesting to me.” The other first-year interrupts. “You know, because my parents are Cambodian refugees. The Khmer Rouge . . .”

“Oh my God, Pol Pot? Was it Pol Pot?”

My important writer pivots away and I stare at the back of her Medusa head of lovely snakes.

The student tells her family’s story. Another genocide. I sip from a goblet of ice water and murmur sympathy, but all I can think about is how I have been eclipsed by this other student. Competitive tragedies. Who has suffered the most? Who has it worse? Who has been more persecuted? Does my resentment mean I am a sociopath?

Of course, the important writer is my mother. No, no, no. Not my real mother. No, a *symbol* of my mother. I want not only her approval, but her love.

In graduate school, I meet someone in the theater department. She designs sets and lights that fade in and out. Not an actress.

She wants to know everything about me. Who are you? She asks. Who are you? “You live behind a scrim.”

Because I love her, I tell her how I survived, though my life was full of unanswered questions. Missing pieces. Absences. Holes. I tell her about my mother. In that house, my grandmother’s house, out seeps tears, grief.

She wants details. Where was I when it happened? I describe the room that day. The pale gold afternoon light was granular; no pixilated, maybe dappled. Walls a muddy shade of pink.

Yes, yes, there is something else. On the wall, a portrait of a woman, her face hidden behind a black veil. A painting or a photograph of a nameless woman. A sepia background? A gray background? The woman in the portrait stares at me. I turn away. Her eyes black holes. Her eyes, my eyes. Black holes. I loathe her. I turn the painting over, her face to the wall, this woman trying to take my mother's place.

In this house, doors slam. My mother opens the window for a cooling breeze.

In this house, my mother disappears.

My lover takes me in her arms. I tell her how while I was growing up, I tried to stay sane, how I was mad with what was called unspecified grief. I tell her I believe my mother is not really gone. How it is possible my mother ran away that day. I am trying to find her, but her identity is scattered. She goes by many names: Anna, Ani, Anahid. Last name Margoian, Hagopian, and Forman. This last one Forman, appeared only once, recorded on my birth certificate.

I tell her how at sixteen, I entered a hospital, a locked unit. How after I was released, I left my grandmother's house.

My lover and I move in together. Our schedules are out of sync because she has hours of rehearsals and I like to write late at night. I go to a little room and write until morning. I'm a poet. I need to be alone to do this.

She complains. The bed we are supposed to share is empty.

"You are abandoning us, you know."

Abandon. The particular word choice is not lost on me, and regrettably my reaction to irony is not a smile exactly, but not a grimace either. This infuriates her. When we finally break up, my lover says. "I don't know you."

I move far away to another coast, another city.

I get a series of day jobs and write poetry. I get a more permanent position and write poetry. I tell my students a refrain is the most important lines in the poem, the ones that keep coming back. And I tell them also refrain means to stop oneself from doing something.

After the towers fall, a critic discovers my poem, "Veil." It is, he posits, a political poem, emblematic of the times we are living in. The word terror takes on a global meaning, not a personal meaning. Isn't everything political, after all? There is no art for art's sake. Doesn't the dome-shaped head evoke the rounded mosque? Is it even a veil? Is it a headscarf? A chador? A burqa? Something pious? Something modest? Something sinister?

Another critic weighs in. No, no, no, it is confessional, borne of trauma. People have leaped from the burning towers after, they have fallen from the sky.

What is my intent? What am I trying to say?

I want no part of any of this. I move out of the city.

Years pass. At sixty, my voice and hair are thinner, my waist thicker, but most remarkably my poem has become well known, and the refrain is often quoted. At any literary event I am invited to, I must of course read "Veil" and nothing else, nothing new.

I'm the Daughter of the Diaspora
I can count to ten.
Meg, yergoo, yereck,
No more
Her eyes black holes.
Black holes unforgetting.
Her eyes, my eyes.
Black holes unforgiving.

On any particular night, the house lights go on, blindingly bright. I search, foolishly, as I always do, for a face that may be my mother's. I scan the front row of wheelchair ladies. But the glare overwhelms me, and I remove my glasses, rub my eyes.

During the Q and A, the handler runs up and down the rows with a microphone. There are a few polite questions about "Veil," the usual ones. "What is the poem saying about the idea of home?" "Is the eye the I?" "What is meant by Diaspora?"

Always the teacher, I turn the questions. What do *you* think is the idea of home? What do *you* think is meant by I?

But eventually the audience hungers for biography. "Your mother.

You never saw her again? Do you know why she did it?"

Don't you see? Don't you see? I want to shout. Here's what I remember. Ally allon axum free. Car horns. Sirens. Here's what I know: I wanted her to find me, unlock the door, release me. But I had to stumble out myself.

Inevitably, someone—many times it's a young woman—asks, "Weren't you angry? Weren't you angry with your mother?" I give a thoughtful pause before I answer, as if I have never before considered this line of inquiry.

"Yes," I say. Or sometimes, "No." It could just as easily be either one. My poor mother.

C. B. Heinemann

An Alpine Hostel

When I landed a summer job at a Swiss youth hostel set in a high Alpine valley, I never imagined that I would end up burying the bodies of several guests in the back under a pile of lichen-coated rocks.

I had just graduated from college and wanted to spend as much time abroad as possible before facing reality and getting a real job. After weeks of traveling through Europe, I found myself in a place where I thought I could be happy for the rest of my life. Ubertal was a hamlet tucked like a tooth filling high in the Berner Oberland mountain range, complete with dizzying views, a small lake, and wooden chalets. With only one tiny road that corkscrewed up from a remote valley below, Ubertal didn't get many visitors other than hikers on the Berner Oberland Circle, a challenging week-long hiking trail. I spent a night at the youth hostel, just outside the village at the foot of a high granite mountain, and met the hostel manager, a guy from Croatia, who spent a year in the States at the same university a former girlfriend of mine attended.

Dany was in his thirties, spoke perfect English, and had been working in Swiss spas and hostels for years. He was a tall, athletic guy with glasses and a crew cut who didn't talk much, but when he did, he had a gentle voice laced with good humor. We sat up late in his office drinking wine and talking about Switzerland. He told me that he also spent time bumming around before getting a job with the Swiss Hostel Federation. When he mentioned that he needed help at the hostel, I jumped on it without hesitation.

My main jobs consisted of cleaning the bathrooms and showers, washing the dishes, and helping to make the beds. I usually had long breaks when I could go on hikes or just hang around. Dany did the cooking, kept track of paperwork, and once or twice a week he would drive down in his VW van to the town of Interlaken to bring up supplies.

Hikers showed up at all hours, usually cranky, footsore, and exhausted, and we provided them with hot meals, showers, and a clean bed. Dany was always the magnanimous host, ready to welcome everyone with a mug of coffee or tea. He spoke some French and pretty good German, which was absolutely necessary, while I struggled to learn enough to get by.

Late one night, he woke me up in my room and handed me a flashlight. "We've had some trouble here tonight and I'll need your help."

I was still halfway in my dream. "What's going on?"

"We've got to go out. And be quiet—we don't want to wake anyone."

"Out?" I pulled on my jeans. "What's the problem?"

"We've got to get rid of something. Something bad."

"Did the septic tank overflow or . . ."

"Worse. Much worse. Somebody died."

I stared up into Dany's face, which was barely illuminated by his flashlight. "Died? What are you frigging talking about? Shouldn't we call an ambulance?"

"Too late for that. He's dead."

I felt a shock ripple through my system as I pulled on my sweater. "Oh crap, how did this happen?"

"We've gotten into something over our heads. We've got to bury the body."

"What we need to do is call the cops." I stopped as horror poured through my system like hot poison. "Someone died here? I can't believe it. Are you sure?"

"Oh, I'm sure." I could detect a tremble in Dany's usually calm voice. "A couple of Russian guys came in late, and they were arguing even as I let them in. They didn't have hiking gear or backpacks or anything. I can understand a little Russian and knew right away we were in trouble. I went into the kitchen to get them some coffee, and I heard them really going at it. By the time I came out to try to calm things down, one of the guys was gone, and the other was slumped over the table—dead. There's no blood so it might be cyanide. Those Russians have a lot of ways to kill each other."

"Murder? Cyanide? Dany, we have to call the cops, man."

"You don't get it." I could see his face harden. "If any of these Russians find out about this, we'll be dead in no time. We've got to get rid of this guy and make it like this never happened."

"Are you crazy? We'll . . ."

"No, you don't understand." He turned to check that the door was locked and lowered his voice to a whisper. "I had no idea the Russian mafia was in Switzerland. Probably just to stash their money in the banks, but they're here. We've got to do this right now." He gave me a look I'd never seen before. "This reminds me of when my family was killed. Years ago."

"My God, your family? Killed?"

"Yeah. Don't ask. Let's do this quick."

I was too groggy, disoriented, and frightened to argue further. Somehow, I decided to do as Dany said and think about it later.

The stars washed across the sky in a brilliant display, and the air was cold as iron. Danny led me outside to a heap of plastic behind the building. "He's in here. I'll take the arms if you'll take the legs . . ."

"There's really a dead guy in this bag? What is it, a body bag?"

"You'd be surprised at what the Swiss Hostel Federation wants us to have on hand just in case. Let's go quickly and be very quiet."

I could never adequately describe my horror and revulsion when I felt those heavy, lifeless legs through the plastic and heaved them up, but I somehow managed to steel myself and do the job. Terror and adrenalin can work wonders, especially when aided by the threat of being murdered, and before I realized it, we had carried the unfortunate man deep into the woods. I could hear the splash of a nearby waterfall.

"I know what to do with him, luckily," said Dany. "There's a hole out here I noticed one day. We can put him in there and cover him with rocks. There are plenty around. But we'll need to be quiet."

We lowered the body into a depression about five feet deep and dropped him at the bottom. I couldn't see exactly what kind of hole it was, but Danny explained that it was formed by ice and water and some kind of reaction to something in the soil. I didn't really understand and was too freaked out to pay attention. Dany lit a lantern that enabled us to find lichen-covered rocks that we could put over the body. They lay all around us in heaps, so we had no trouble finding more than enough to fill the hole. It took a while, but at last the job was done and the grave just looked like any other pile of stones in the woods.

"All right, that's good," Dany said. "Well, not good, I know. Horrible, really. But I don't think anyone will ever find him."

I was throbbing with terror. "Who's going to look for him? What if the Russians come up here looking for him and decide to kill us?"

"Nobody except his killer will ever know he was here, and he won't talk. He was killed in a place nobody would ever think the Russian mafia would be. An obscure Alpine hostel catering to hikers? No, the idea was probably to assassinate this guy in a place where nobody would know who or what he was."

"This is frigging insane! How did we get mixed up in all this?"

"Bad luck. Anyway, let's get going, and be really quiet. The last thing we need is for somebody to see us creeping out of the woods."

"Holy shit . . ."

"Be sure to wash any traces of the woods out of your hands, clothes, shoes. And do it in your room so nobody sees you."

As we stumbled through the dark under that vast expanse of stars, I struggled to breathe. I never realized how blameless my life had been until that night. But that was over. I was now covering up a murder and would have to keep that ghastly secret forever.

Once locked in my room, I scrubbed my hands, shoes, and face. I lay down in bed, clutching my Swiss Army knife just in case. I knew I wouldn't sleep that night. My stomach churned and my brain was racing. As soon as it was light, I told myself, I'll leave this place forever.

But I didn't leave. I had to help Dany make breakfast for twenty hikers who wanted to get an early start, and then wash the dishes, clean the bathrooms, and change the beds. It was gorgeous day, the granite peaks soaring clear against the blue sky, the air outside laced with the fragrance of wood smoke and so fresh it stung my lungs to breath it. Already my mind was pushing the events of the previous night into a little box in the far reaches of my consciousness. It all seemed like a bad dream, and I wondered if maybe it actually had been a dream. I watched Dany, who seemed like his usual benevolent self, handing out plates of food, offering advice in his Croatian-accented German, making sure everyone had enough coffee. Yes, I thought, it was all a dream. A terrible, vivid dream.

And so it went for the next couple of weeks. In spite of fear and common sense, I stayed at the hostel with Dany, taking care of guests, working at my chores, and pushing the incident further back in my mind. I was actually more afraid of leaving than staying, though if you had asked me why I couldn't have come up with any explanation. Although we never spoke about what happened, there was a bond between Dany and me that was as powerful as it was dreadful. We had to stick together—it was us against the world now. So, I stayed there with Dany and bit by bit tried to scrub that night from my mind.

In late July, the meadow next to the hostel exploded with wildflowers, the weather was perfect, and the hostel hummed with activity. People from all over the world looking for a secluded Alpine nook managed to find us, and we made new friends every day. We had fondue nights on

Tuesdays, raclette on Fridays, and many hikers planned their routes to be there on one or more of those nights.

One day, we got a special envelope from the Swiss Hostel Federation. Dany and I both felt apprehensive about it, so we decided to open it that night after everyone had gone to sleep. At about eleven o'clock, we withdrew into his office.

"I always get a little nervous when these letters arrive," said Dany as he pulled open the flap. "You never know when they might just decide to close you down. They're always looking to save money."

As he read the contents to me, I realized that our fears were way off-track. "They're giving us a raise—a big one," said Danny with a grin, his eyes wide under those glasses. "And that's not all."

"What is it?"

He shoved the letter over to me. "You must know a little German by now."

"Come on, man, what does it say?"

He lunged up and hurried into the kitchen, returning with a bottle of Mumm's champagne and two fluted plastic glasses.

"Come on, Dany, what is it?"

"Ski slopes are opening up just down the road." He sat back in his chair and pulled out the cork, that grin still in place. "They want to keep the hostel open all year for the skiers. This is it—we're an all-year operation. And making more money. Can you believe it? I guess you brought us luck when I hired you."

The news didn't feel so great to me. I wondered if I'd ever be able to get away while Dany poured champagne. "Awesome. Just awesome."

Our next paychecks alleviated my gloom considerably—I was making more than I would have made back home. In fact, I had quite a nice bank account saved up. I only worked a couple of hours a day while the rest of my time was spent hanging out with our guests or going on hikes of my own. Except for having to get up at dawn, it was the perfect life.

On a cloudless afternoon I was returning from a hike up *Teufeltal*, a narrow valley between two mountain ranges that was a wonderland of waterfalls and Alpine tundra. Dany was waiting for me, pacing back and forth behind the building. I felt a shock of fear burn through my system.

"Come on, man!" he shouted. "Come to the cellar, quick!"

I ran down and followed him through the storm door to our cellar, which we used to dry clothes and store wine. There on the floor lay a man in a green parka. He had longish dark hair and stubble on his face. I looked at Dany while my heart took a nosedive. "Is he dead?"

"I'm afraid so." He tried to lift the man's arm. "Stiff as a board. No sign of blood. We've got to get him out of here." He put his hand on my shoulder. "This is the Russian guy who killed the first one."

My thoughts sped up and scrambled my brain. "Look, Dany, we've got to get the police here—this is insane—we can't live like this, covering up murders, burying people in the woods!"

Dany walked to the corner and picked up a large black plastic bag. "I still have one more, can you believe it?"

"We're not doing this, Dany. This is for the police, not for us. I don't need two dead guys on my conscience. I'll lose my mind . . ."

"You'll lose more than that if we get the cops involved. Our faces will end up in the papers. Next thing you know, the Russian mafia will make it their business to shut us up permanently. Either that or they'll frame us for it—that's something they're good at. Whatever happens, this hostel would be closed down and we'll be out of a job—that's the best-case scenario."

"We can get other jobs."

"But we can't get other lives." He held up the bag. "We've got to do this. We have no choice, I told you."

"But by doing this we're working for them, don't you see? We're their body disposal unit! I don't want to be a criminal."

"You don't get it. If we say a thing, we're dead."

"Reporting a dead body can't get us killed."

"You don't know these guys. They've got ears everywhere."

"I haven't seen a damned thing except this guy."

"They don't know that. They'll kill us without a second thought. Come on, we've got to do this before anyone gets back."

The terror in Dany's eyes swayed me more than his words. As if in another dimension, I helped him pull the guy into the bag and zip it up. As we did, I saw a piece of paper poking out of the man's coat pocket. For reasons I'll never understand, I snatched the paper and stuffed it into my back pocket while Dany wasn't looking.

Dany opened the storm door a crack. "Crap, we can't take him in broad daylight—someone will see us. We'll have to wait until tonight."

The rest of that day I felt so stressed that I could barely function. My fingers twitched and I felt sick to my stomach. Somehow, I managed to get the dinner dishes washed and retired to my room where I lay in bed trying to slow my breathing.

After an eternity, I heard a knock on the door. It was time. "I got everybody booked into rooms on the other side of the building so they can't see us," Dany said. "But we should move fast."

I was numb as we picked up the bag and carried it into the woods. Dany managed to find another depression in the ground even deeper in the woods where we lay the body, again covered it with big rocks, tossed handfuls of leaves over it, and started back.

That numbness continued into the next day. I did my chores on automatic pilot and hurried to my room at the end of the day. No hike, no scrabble or guitar playing with the guests. I couldn't sleep that night because I was listening to every sound, every movement, expecting some Russians to pay us a late night visit.

Just before dawn, I pulled out that piece of paper I took from the dead man's pocket. On it was something written in black ink in a foreign language. "That looks like Dany's handwriting," I murmured. "I must be losing my mind. What the hell is it?" I turned the paper over and noticed, peeking from the one torn corner, what looked to me like the emblem of the Swiss Hostel Federation. "Can't be," I muttered.

I pulled out a sheaf of Federation writing paper from the desk in my room and looked at the emblem on my paper, and then the emblem on the Russians' paper. "Jesus, it looks the same. It is the same. But, damn, Dany sure as hell wouldn't be writing letters to these guys. This is crazy. It had to be somebody else. But who?"

Nobody came that night, but I knew they would eventually. Something held me to that terrible place and I didn't know how to break the spell.

One day an Irish girl arrived with pink cheeks, gleaming dark hair, and a clever sense of humor. Marion was traveling after graduating from university and was interested in how the hostel ran. We suggested some day hikes, and in the evening, she hung out in the kitchen to talk.

"You lads have a grand life up here," she said while I washed the dinner dishes. "I could see staying up here, away from it all. Here, let me give you a hand."

"No, I'll take care of it. You just relax. Anyway, what you're saying is what I thought when I came here, and now look at me," I said, aware of the irony in my words. "Wearing an apron, catering to the leisure classes."

She laughed. "You could do worse." Her blue eyes flashed. "Need any more help up here? Ski season is just around the corner."

"I'll ask Dany. I think it would be great to have you."

As much as I would have loved for Marion to become a permanent fixture in my life, I couldn't bear to see her life ruined by those murders. I decided not to ask Dany, noting bitterly that I was now lying to a beautiful girl because of our predicament.

That evening, we sat by the fire with some white Chasselas wine from the shores of Lake Geneva. Marion brought out a concertina and played jigs and reels for the other guests while I tried to back her up on the hostel guitar. It was a magical evening, and after everyone else had gone to bed the two of us sat together talking until nearly two in the morning.

Marion was everything I had ever dreamed of in a girl—beautiful, funny, smart, talented. Like me, after finishing college she was avoiding the working world, unlike most of her classmates who had already inserted themselves into jobs, mortgages, and families. "I'm still young, and I want to see the world and have adventures," she said. "I'm not quite ready to put on the hair shirt and hunch over a computer for the next thirty years."

"I know exactly what you mean. That's how I ended up here."

"Besides, what kind of job could I get? I majored in Slavic languages. Not the best way to get a high paying job, is it?"

"It'll probably help you more than my English degree can help me."

She moved closer. "So, what do you want to do with your life?"

"Ever since I got here, I can't remember." I thought of that piece of paper. "Hey, I'd like to show you something."

I ran to my room, took the paper from the bottom of my sock drawer, and brought it to Marion. "Can you read whatever this is?"

She held the paper—I immediately regretted putting something connected with something so terrible into her lovely hands—and looked it over with a half-smile. "Yes, no problem. It's in Serbo-Croatian"

"What does it say?"

"It's directions on how to get here. Somebody probably left it behind."

I sat down, feeling so dizzy that I thought I might pass out. "Yes, I'm sure that's what happened."

"What's the matter?"

"Nothing, nothing at all. Just a little tired, that's all."

To my surprise, she leaned over and kissed my lips. Then she stood up. "You'd better get some sleep, and I don't want to keep you up."

"I don't mind not sleeping, believe me. I've been doing a lot of that lately."

"We'll talk later. I just signed up for another week." She flashed a smile and turned. "Maybe I'll never get out of here, either."

As I lay in bed that night, my mind was churning. Why would Dany, or anyone, send Russian gangsters directions to the hostel? A thousand excuses jammed themselves into my thoughts. That wasn't Dany's handwriting—it was just slightly similar.

But the question that kept sleep away was—who used Hostel Federation paper to give those guys directions to our hostel?

When I got up early the next day, Marion wasn't around. After cleaning, I took a hike up to Steinmeer, a high lake surrounded by snowy peaks. Marion had mentioned something about going there, but when I arrived, I was the only person around. The first snow of the season began to fall, turning the high Alps into a white wonderland.

The weather can swiftly turn nasty in the higher altitudes, so I decided I'd better head back. About a quarter of a mile from the hostel, I heard branches rustling, and Dany burst out and onto the trail. "I didn't think you'd be up here," he said.

"Oh no, no." I knew that look on his face.

"Yes, another Russian. I could use a little help getting more rocks. I had to drag him here myself."

"How did you do it?"

"I put him into a plastic airline bag I used for my backpack, stuffed him into my van, and drove up the fire trail."

In spite of the snow, I sat down on the path. "I can't go on like this. We'll have half the population of Europe buried back here if this . . ."

"This is the last. They left a note."

He reached into his pocket and pulled out a folded sheet of paper. I took it in my cold-stiffened fingers and opened it. Inside was a message in block letters. *Sorry for the trouble. We won't be back.*

"That was taped to his forehead," Dany explained. "I found him in the cellar."

A surge of vomit shot from my mouth and onto the pristine snow. "God, I can't do this anymore," I gasped as I struggled to breathe.

"This is the end of it, believe me."

With resignation and despair, I followed Dany into the woods, stepping over the rocks and pushing aside vines so that the snow that had landed on them shivered, scattered, and fell in clouds like ashes. We walked for a long way, crossing two half-frozen streams, until we arrived at a small pile of stones. "I can't take this anymore," I said. "I'm leaving tomorrow."

After tossing more rocks onto the pile, we walked to Dany's van without a word. We made a simple meal of potatoes and cheese for our handful of dinner guests. I stayed in the kitchen so that I wouldn't have to talk to anyone, but I could see Marion sitting at her laptop, hard at work on something. Finally, depressed beyond anything I had ever known, I escaped to my bed.

Early the next morning, I shuffled into the kitchen. It was still dark outside. Nothing was on the stove; the coffee machine was unplugged.

"What the hell?" I knocked on Dany's door but got no answer. "Time to get breakfast going, then I'm out of here for good." Still no answer. At last, I pushed his door open and looked in. The bed was made and all his belongings were gone. A note was lying on the bed in the same handwriting that I'd seen on the note in the Russian's pocket. I picked it up with trembling fingers. *Sorry for all the trouble. Those men were not Russian. They were Serbs. They were the men who killed my family back in Croatia during the war. Now I must leave. Good luck to you, my friend.*

The revelation gushed through me like a choking torrent of poison. "Those men we buried killed his family. He even gave them directions here. It was all right in front of me. I am a complete and utter idiot."

"I could have told you that." I turned to see Marion's sleepy face smiling at me. Her eyes sparkled and her hair was wonderfully disheveled. "Hey, what's the matter?"

"Dany's gone," I said, working to maintain my composure. "He's been having some, ah, personal problems. I should have seen this coming long ago."

"I heard him say he was going back home, but I didn't know it was today."

"You knew he was leaving?"

"You didn't know? I heard him on the phone last night. Talking in Serbo-Croatian.'

I felt dizzy. "What was he saying?"

"Something about how he tied up some unfinished business. Something about his family years ago."

"His family? Unfinished business?"

"He was also kind enough to pull some strings and get me a job at the hostel on Inishmore, on the Aran Islands off the west coast of Ireland. You too, if you want it. I was surprised that he did that. But really, I'd rather stay here. With you."

The bloody fingers of the Balkan War had crawled across the years all the way to our secluded little hostel. He killed those men, and I helped him hide the bodies. Without knowing it I had taken part in three murders. Those bodies rotting out in the Alpine forest were partly my responsibility.

"Oh, still, it's a shame, him leaving you like this." Marion pushed her hair back from her face. "So, you'll be needing some help with breakfast, I'm guessing."

"I need to call the Hostel Federation."

Marion threw herself against me and hugged hard. Her hair smelled like jasmine. "I'm sorry about your friend, but I'll stay and help you."

Another black flood of horror filled my spirit. "I loved it here, at least in the beginning. But we have to leave."

Marion looked into my face, her eyes swarming with confusion. "Why? Don't you still love it here?"

I glanced out the window at the dark woods behind the hostel. Tears felt like they scalded my eyes and burned their way down my face. "I can't stay, and neither can you. I'll explain it to you someday. Once we

get away from here. We'll have to get some new people here. I'll make a call and it'll only take a couple of days."

"But will you come to Inishmore with me?"

"Yes, Marion, yes. Thank you. And it can't be soon enough."

Very early the next week, I walked with Marion to the bus stop just across the road. She was more subdued than usual, and there wasn't much I could say. After one last look at our hostel, the bus heaved up a hill before making the long, zig-zag descent down the mountains to the town of Martigny, where the Rhone River makes a dramatic turn on its journey south to the Mediterranean. The hikers had already gone after we served them one last breakfast, and a new hostel manager had already arrived. A brief rain skittered overhead from the mountaintops, so I gave Marion a kiss and took her hand as we made our way to the valley far below.

Jeff McLaughlin

Marriage

"They're unexpectedly running late," my wife said. She clicked the phone back into its cradle.

"Sweet mercy," I said, clapping my hand to my chest and feigning heart palpitations. I staggered towards her. "But Kyle's never late," I said. "Never, ever late. Five minutes early is late. I've heard that fifteen times if I've heard it once. And we only see them twice a year."

Charlotte stood with one hand on her hip, the other resting on the counter. She drummed her thin fingers and raised her eyebrows in mostly mock irritation.

"I think the way you're looking at me means I should apologize," I said. "Or perhaps," I said, snapping my fingers and pointing at her, "that I should be nice because she's your oldest friend. Or," I said, and then I repeated, with enthusiasm, "orrrrr, it means we have time to run upstairs and you know, snuggle a bit before they get here."

"They're only a little behind," she said. She took two steps towards me and patted my shoulder. "Maybe if you were still in your twenties, though, you'd be fast enough."

"Touché," I said. I kissed her forehead. I watched her move around the kitchen. Faint gray streaked her blonde hair, which was drawn from her face in much the same fashion it had been thirty years earlier, and in some fundamental way she seemed, to me, despite everything, to be ageless.

She caught me staring. "What?" she asked.

"I was just thinking you are as appealing as any woman I have ever seen."

"We don't have time," she insisted. She leaned towards me and wagged her finger.

"No, really," I said. "That's really what I was thinking. You're the one who made it lascivious."

"Well, in that case, I appreciate it, despite your need to impress me with big words."

"I do what I can," I said. "So, I know you've told me about thirty times. But why are they driving through?"

"To. Visit. Their. Daughter. In. College," she said. "In this very city."

"Yes, yes," I said.

She sighed and looked out the window.

"A penny for your thoughts," I said.

"Oh," she said. "I was trying to decide if I loved you despite your absentmindedness, or because of it."

"Let's go with because," I said. "That seems best for all involved."

She came close to me again, and this time she patted my cheek as she might some distracted child. "Best for you, anyway," she said. She started out of the room.

"Hey," I said. I waited for her to turn around. "I love you," I said.

"Likewise," she said. "You're fulfilling your promise to make me laugh, anyway." Then she was gone.

They were exactly seven minutes late. I know this because I watched the clock intently, wondering what it would be like to be so locked to precision. It was unhappily stressful. But then their car pulled into the drive, and Lori climbed out. She was dressed, as she always was, as they both always were, too formally. She'd been friends with my wife since their junior year in college, when they studied abroad together. That meant she had known my wife longer than I. The two women hugged on the sidewalk.

Kyle, Lori's husband, came around the car, the ruler-straight creases in his pants unbroken by movement. We shook hands. "Sorry we're late," he said.

"No worries," I said.

"That's your mantra," he said, and he clapped me on the shoulder as if we were old friends, true friends, rather than forced acquaintances.

"I guess it's one of them," I said.

He leaned down to hug Charlotte. She kissed him on the cheek. I gave Lori a little wave.

"Come in, come in," my wife said. She led the way, with Lori close behind her, then Kyle, and then me.

We stood around the kitchen counter and asked innocuous questions and told pleasant stories about our children. The green lights of the oven clock glared at me. I watched them shift, minute by minute, and felt like a kid trapped at school on a beautiful day. Some section of the conversation drifted past me. The mention of a dog brought me back.

"A new dog," Kyle said, scornfully. "At our age."

"The girls are gone," she said. "Wouldn't it be nice to have companionship around the house."

"Do you want another dog?" I asked Charlotte.

"Oh, we'd never do as well a second time," she said.

"What was the name of your dog?" Kyle asked.

Charlotte rolled her eyes. "I almost can't bear to say it aloud," she said.

"What?" I asked, feigning obliviousness. We had let the two girls each give it a name, with a predictable result.

"Dorothy Angel," my wife said.

Lori almost laughed but then glanced at Kyle and stopped. Then, unexpectedly, the laugh reemerged and trilled out.

"It's okay to laugh," I said. "Shit, I laughed about it all the time. The girl down the street named hers Butterfluff. Granted, it looks like a Butterfluff, but I still laugh at that."

Kyle shook his head and looked down. "What?" Lori asked.

"Doesn't it ever bother you?" he asked. He looked at each of us. "How permissive you were?"

"Letting our kids name their own dog?" Charlotte asked.

"Just everything," he said. "What if they had chosen something completely inappropriate?"

"I don't know," I said. "We would have steered them back to something else."

"I remember when one of your two girls announced she could spell 'toot,'" he said. "When she was about four years old. Right here. In this very room. And that you taught her," he said, pointing at me.

"She asked," I said. "She asked how to spell it and I told her."

"I'm not sure I agreed with that decision," Charlotte said.

"Well, she would have figured it out on her own, eventually," I said. "Or worse, some kid on the playground would have misinformed her. I mean, ignorance is never good, right?"

Kyle looked at Lori. I tried to read her face. I was intentionally goading him. I will admit to that. Charlotte's comment was intended to make me stop. But I had some irrational notion that Lori was secretly urging me on. Her head was gently tilted, as if she was considering something slightly different than the rest of us. I glanced at Charlotte, who also studied her old friend, as if awaiting judgement. Charlotte had always looked up to her, despite their similar ages. This went back, I believe, to their initial levels of confidence when they had first met.

Thirty years ago, Lori had been strikingly beautiful, and now, despite the tolls of age, she still carried herself with an antiquated assurance. It seemed sad to me, misplaced. It's not that she had aged poorly, more that she had settled. A vague heaviness draped over her form, strikingly apparent compared to Charlotte, for whom fitness was important. A stranger might have guessed she was a decade older than my wife.

The room had gone silent for ten full seconds. "Lori?" Kyle finally asked.

"What?" Lori asked back.

"I want to know what you think," Kyle said.

She sighed. She set her glass on the slate end table. It made a scraping clink. "I think that was a long time ago," she said.

"We used to shake our heads about that dog and its stupid name," he said. "We used to agree that not everything was a joke. Do you remember?"

"Of course, I remember that," she said. "But it was a long time ago. Does it matter anymore?"

I had not stopped watching Lori, for reasons I cannot articulate. I felt Charlotte shift and turned to her. She had an unspoken plea on her face, to make it better, to end this scene, but carefully.

"So," I said. I stood. I brushed my hands together the way people do when they have completed something in a satisfactory manner. "I'll go fire up the grill."

"Oh, good idea," Charlotte said. "Please do. We should get dinner started."

"Anyone need anything, while I'm up?" I asked.

"No, thank you," Lori said. She looked away from me when she spoke. She stared at some vague space in the middle of the air.

"I'll come join you in a minute," Kyle said.

"That'd be great," I said, with all the enthusiasm I could manufacture. Charlotte smiled at me. For the moment, all was well.

I started scraping the metal grate with the rusted wire brush. Kyle came out and looked around the yard.

"I've always liked this place," he said.

"Us, too," I said. "And we lucked out with our neighbors."

"Hmm," Kyle said. He was thinking about something else. I can honestly tell you I knew I had no idea what he might be considering.

Even so, he still managed to surprise me. "Can they hear us in there?" he asked.

I looked through the open window. Charlotte had turned on some music and it trickled out, behind the clink of their glasses, their separate conversation, carried along in light tones. "I doubt it," I said.

He looked around surreptitiously. His body seemed to coil upon itself. It made me uneasy. So I hunched my shoulders and held the spatula as one might a dagger, ready to defend against this unknown, yet unperceived threat. But he refused to respond to that. "Are you happy you married Charlotte?" he asked me. He frowned as he spoke.

"Kyle," I said. I tapped the brush against the grate for emphasis. "I don't suppose we're close enough friends for you to ask me that."

He shook his head. "Who else can I ask?"

"Well," I said. "I guess if you're asking, over the course of twenty-six years of marriage, if I have ever thought about what my life would be like without her, then, yes. But I'm happy I married her, and I'm happy we're still married."

"You don't ever think of anyone else?"

I bit my tongue. I mean this literally. I squeezed the tip of my tongue between my front teeth until it hurt. "Why are you asking me this?" I finally said.

He raised his glass so quickly a little sloshed onto the patio. "Because, well, take this the right way, but you don't seem like the faithful type."

"That's a hard thing to take the right way, Kyle," I said. "I'm also not sure why it would seem true to you."

"You know," he said. "Always joking, never taking anything too seriously. You're artsy in your own way. Charlotte seems like she'd forgive anything."

"No," I said. "I've never thought of anyone else. Not once."

I lied. Not only had I thought about cheating on Charlotte, I'd done it. Not in the way or for a reason someone like Kyle would expect. But about nine years earlier, the girls were eleven and thirteen, and Charlotte found a lump. Initially it had not been overly alarming. But it proved to be cancerous. The doctors used phrases like preparing for the worst, and palliative care. In the days before her surgery, I lay awake in bed consoling and comforting her, even while I was dreading life without her. I'd be overwhelmed beyond imagining. A job, the girls, a dead wife, buried. Alone, very alone, and too busy to ever stop being alone.

She stayed in the hospital the night before the operation. Our girls went to stay with my parents. Charlotte's parents came to our house to look after their daughter. I wondered how long I would want them to stay, how I would care for the girls without them.

But the surgery went smoothly, despite all initial indications the disease was contained, she would be fine, it was not a miracle, not exactly, but unexpected and wonderful, absolutely. We smiled and hugged, and I left her there to recover. I was supposed to go directly home, to relax, to sleep. I did not.

I stopped at a bar, something I had never done before nor done since in my entire married life. I had a drink, leaning back and watching some random game on a massive television. I drank slowly. I considered my life, our house and kids and successes and thought that nothing I did, no action I took, had any consequence at all. I had done nothing to make Charlotte sick, and I had done nothing to make her better. I had another drink.

It would be too easy to say I was drunk. I was not. Perhaps I was impaired. Perhaps some self-definition, some resilience, had been weakened. The sudden absence of despair was strangely disconcerting. I hovered in a perplexing middle place.

Did I notice her first, or she me? It doesn't matter, though for some inexplicable reason I wish I knew. I remember her name, Heather, that she also had two daughters, that she was divorced, that her boyfriend had just left her to go back to his wife, and that she was staying in some tiny apartment trying to figure out what she was going to do next. She was a small person, she seemed like a delicate person. It might be unfathomable to you that on the night after I learned Charlotte, whom I loved, would live, that I would be fumbling around with a strange woman in the back seat of her car. But that's what happened.

By the time I got home my in-laws were asleep. I had to take off my shoes to sneak through my own house. I could not bear to look at myself in the mirror. I showered in the dark.

In the morning, they said nothing about my absence nor my return. Perhaps they never noticed. Perhaps in their own relief they were blind to everything.

I drove over to see Charlotte. Someone had tied a bandanna over her bare head. It looked uncomfortable. I stood in the doorway and studied her for a moment and tried to decide what, if anything, I would tell her, then, or ever. Her face lay turned towards the window. I could not see if she was awake.

"Hey," I called, softly. I felt like crying. It was all I could do to not cry. Though me crying at that moment would have made no sense to her.

She rolled her head. Her eyes widened and she smiled. "Hey," she said. Her voice was scratchy, nearly unintelligible.

"Still all good news?" I asked.

"Still all good news," she confirmed. She nodded towards the chair beside the bed, and I sat and leaned forward and took her small, dry hand in my own. "I was just lying here thinking," she rasped. "You know what I was thinking? I was thinking we need to just laugh more. We get worked up about useless things. We're not going to starve. We'll pay off our house. It's ok if we don't go to London every year. All of that is silliness. Promise me we'll just laugh more," she said. "Promise me from now on, we'll laugh."

I sat there. I was crying, though not for the reason she thought. "All right," I said. "I promise."

She squeezed my hand. "You were always the guy who made me laugh. I got lucky. Let's live inside that, all right?"

I nodded. I sat beside her and nodded. I thought that our first life was over and that a second one was starting right that moment. She gently squeezed my fingers. I closed my eyes.

So, nine years later, as I stood there listening to Kyle ask me if I had thought about adultery, I considered how he might see things. A world of absolutes. A world in which everything was consequential. A world in which he had to be certain to be happy. He was brittle. This made me pity him.

"Well," he said. "Anyway."

"Anyway, indeed," I said. I turned back to the grill. I tried to think of something to make him feel better. "It's ok to think bad things now and then," I said, without looking at him, trying to offer some consolation. But he had already started back inside.

I scarcely talked through dinner, content to listen to Charlotte and Lori review familiar stories, to hear about their daughters, to clear the table and pour coffee and wait for the evening to dissolve away. Though I did think, while I waited, that there was a time, when I was younger, when I would have looked at her, or their life, their greater wealth, with envy. Not anymore. The satisfaction of coming this far with Charlotte, through illness, with our daughters, that satisfaction means everything.

Even so I found myself staring at Lori, this pleasant human being, who had married a man who was now considering cheating on her. She is a physically quiet person. When she was younger it had been a key part of her grace, though now it had begun to suggest lethargy. It took some time, that much time, for me to notice the blue wristband she wore.

"Hey," I said, when conversation lagged. I pointed. "Is that one of those step counters?"

"Yes," she said. "It is." She smiled, turning her attention to me. "I just got it. I'm changing my life."

"I don't need anyone tracking what I'm doing all day long," Kyle said. "Freaks at some company. Who knows what they do with the data?"

"There's a huge black market for step counts," I said. "Enormous. Credit cards, social security numbers, step counts, you know."

"You joke," he said. "But you don't have one."

"I don't need one for tennis," I said. This represented a meaningless truth. I had a racquet and balls and on occasion went to the courts, though not frequently enough to support my authoritative implication. Charlotte was eyeing me again, forehead creased, warning.

"How does it work?" Charlotte asked. I kept my eyes on Lori. I was avoiding looking at Kyle, since he had settled back to his usual position, which was under my skin.

"Oh, I don't know, exactly," Lori said. "But every time I move it picks it up somehow. It's fun to sync it and look at the charts. Some girls at work set up a group so we can compete."

"Could you attach it to your new dog and have it run around?" I asked.

"That would be cheating," she exclaimed. "Though I'm sure someone could."

"Seems about right," Kyle said.

"Excuse me?" I asked.

"Oh, like we were talking about earlier," he said. "You don't take anything too seriously. Why not cheat?"

There is no way he could have known. The word still hurt. No one knows except for one woman I saw one night nearly a decade ago. Something I had never told my wife because I had promised to make her laugh forever forward. It was a lucky stab. But it stilled me to silence. Charlotte watched me. She thought I was not responding because I was trying to remain polite. But I was not responding because I was frightened of what

I would say, or even do.

So instead, I stood. "Well," I announced, "gotta scrape off the grill before it sets up."

"Oh, yes, do that," Charlotte said. I refilled my coffee cup and stepped outside into the pleasant night. I could see my neighbors sitting on their own porch. I raised my cup in greeting and they called out a quiet good evening. Then Kyle came out. I turned to him. I expected an apology. I nearly got one, until he ruined it.

"I'm sorry," he said. "Things just get to me. You both have always been so damn relaxed about everything. Maybe because you've had it easy in life. But when something tough comes your way, or your kids' way, how will they handle it? All this joking around," he concluded, without any conclusion.

Despite my preexisting disdain for him, this was the first time it had ever transformed into real animosity. Possibly he had forgotten that Charlotte was supposed to have died. Possibly he hadn't considered the countless other things, large and small, that had interrupted our lives as they interrupt those of every human being. Possibly it was that our success in moving past difficulties while remaining in love is something I consider a great accomplishment, which he willfully perceived as weakness, and while I would like to think I don't care about his judgment, at that moment I did.

The shift to our daughters confused me, at first, but as I worked over the grill, I thought about it. His older daughter had gone to the little college where he worked and she now had a job as a secretary, despite some glorified title. She lived with her boyfriend in a studio apartment. Perhaps he thought that job was beneath her. Our eldest had a job lined up in a moderately prestigious art gallery.

"Well," I said. "I think we tried to raise them to be flexible and kind and to work hard. That's all you can really do as parents, don't you think?"

"My parents raised me right. Lori and I raised our kids the same way," he said. "We called my father the General, you know. We knew how to follow rules." He sat, appearing satisfied that this little story had conveyed something conclusive. I considered, for a brief moment, that he might know something about our daughters that I did not. But they were on opposite coasts, far from us, far from him. I hung the brush off the side of the grill and wrestled on the cover.

He swirled his drink and looked up. "What happened to your tree?"

"The split part? The tornado last summer, same one that hit the college."

"Not here. That was further west. It would have been straight line winds here," he said.

I looked at the tree and back at him. "Does it matter?" I asked.

"Yes," he said.

The two women came back outside and saved me from whatever I might have said next.

"Oh," Lori said. "I always forget how nice your porch is. Isn't it, Kyle?"

"It's very nice," he said.

"What were you two talking about?" Charlotte asked.

"Oh, cultural contrasts," I said. "I mean, would you rather live with a bunch of godless heathens like the Swedes, or moral fanatics like in Iran?"

"Well," Charlotte said. "I haven't been either place, but I'd have to go with the Swedes."

"Agreed," Lori said.

"That's not precisely what we were discussing," Kyle said.

"We should go to Sweden," I said to Charlotte." We should go in July and stay awake for 23 hours and watch the sun go around the sky."

"What are you talking about?" Kyle asked.

"The sun," I said. "That close to the North Pole, in the summer, it makes a ring around the horizon. It never really sets. Or so I'm told. I've never been there, either."

"Horizon," Lori giggled. This surprised me, and Charlotte, as well. We both stared at her.

"What's so funny?" Charlotte asked.

"Kyle can't tell the difference between horizontal and vertical," she said. "I mean, he can't remember which is which."

"Why would you say that?" Kyle asked.

"It's true," Charlotte said.

It doesn't matter," I said. "He can absolutely tell the difference between right and wrong." I regretted this immediately. We had reached a point in conversation when things might have drifted back towards amity.

"You see?" Kyle said to Lori, as if he had been awaiting something just like this. "He takes nothing seriously." He looked at Charlotte. "I don't know how you stay married to him."

“Every marriage is a mystery,” Charlotte said. She reached over and grasped my hand. “Sometimes even to the people within it.’

My God did I love her right then.

We watched them drive away. I did not wave until they had backed out of the driveway and only Lori could see me. We stood on the steps until their car vanished beneath the trees and into the night. I followed Charlotte inside, closed the door, and leaned against it. She paused in the foyer.

“Do you remember how big this house seemed when we first moved in?” I asked.

She shook her head, slightly, not in answer to the question, but because I had startled her out of whatever thought she was pursuing.

“Before we had furniture, you mean?”

“Before we had anything,” I said. “When it was all empty. It felt huge. It felt like more space than we could ever fill. And now, now, look at how crowded it is.”

“It’s not crowded,” she said. “It’s full. It’s full of our life together.”

“That’s exactly it,” I said.

“You distracted me,” she teased, and poked my arm. ‘You totally distracted me.”

“I meant to. This time, anyway,” I said. “Why don’t you head upstairs, and I’ll finish cleaning up.”

“Husband of the year award,” she said.

“Twenty-five of the last twenty-six years,” I said.

“Or something,” she said, but she squeezed my arm and kissed my cheek.

I locked the front door. I straightened a few things in the kitchen. I glanced outside for the last time. Diffused yellow light fell from our bedroom window onto the lawn. I decided not to say anything about Kyle’s questions. I was done thinking about him until he made his inevitable return. I was grateful they were staying in a hotel. I was grateful to be alone with my wife in our house.

When I came upstairs, she was already in a t-shirt and pajama pants, arched over the counter, studying her own face in the mirror.

“Like what you see?” I asked. “Because I do,” I said. I sat on the bed where I could watch her.

She leaned back to look at me. “You’re sweet,” she said.

"I am," I agreed. "You're a very lucky woman."

"I'll be sure to tell all my friends," she said. Her voice was strained because she was tugging on her skin.

"You do that," I said. "In case you get hit by a bus I want them to all know how wonderful I'd be."

"Right," she said. "Riiiiiight. So, anyway," she continued. "How do you think they were?"

"Same as always, I guess," I said. "They both seem tired. So stressed. It must be exhausting. It's just that, well, Kyle's such a pain in the ass," I said. "Sorry. I know he's your friend's husband."

"Well," she said. "You might be rid of him soon. Divorce is in the future. The near future," she said, and looked at me. "I give them a couple of months, at best."

"Why do you think that?" I asked. "Did she say something to you?"

"Oh, heavens no," Charlotte said. She smiled. "She'd no more tell me that directly than you could keep a secret from me."

"I see," I said.

"It's just little things I noticed," Charlotte said. "Something's shifted between them. They've never been warm and fuzzy people, but there's something extra, now."

"He annoys me so damn much," I said, "that the only thing I notice is how slowly time moves when he's around."

"Well," Charlotte said, smiling a subtle smile. "When it happens, we'll have to act sad and surprised for her. No one wants to be told the cracks in their marriage were visible. At least not right away."

"Huh," I said. I lolled my head back. I noticed that dust had collected on the front edges of the ceiling fan blades. How this accumulates baffles me.

"You're already thinking about something else," she accused, teasing.

"Momentarily distracted, is all," I said. "He asked me some bizarre question about me cheating on you," I said. "I didn't think he meant anything by it."

"Hmmmm," she said. "I wonder if it's already happened."

"Not on his side, I don't think," I said. "He's too sure of himself. Too righteous."

"We'll know one day," she said. "Besides, the too righteous are the first to stray."

"I'm glad you think that," I said. "You of all people can confirm my abject lack of righteousness."

She finished in the bathroom, switched off the light, and lay beside me.

"So, I need to ask you something important," I said.

Her face scrunched up and she looked closely at me, to be sure I was serious. "Anything," she said, softly.

"They travel more than we do, have more money, better cars, you name it. You ever get jealous?"

"No."

"Not even a little bit?"

She eased around to look more closely at me. "No," she repeated. "Never once, not for a moment. You've stood by me, you've stood by our daughters, you've always done everything for us. I don't give a fuck about anything else. All right?"

"All right," I said. I started to smile.

"Don't laugh at me when I swear. It means I mean it."

"It's funny," I insisted. "I'm sorry. I love you. I love you as much as anyone could love another person."

"I know," she said. We lay there. I could smell the soap from her face. I felt the bones of her chest against my ribs. From behind them I could feel her heart beat. I could feel her breath on my skin. There was nothing more I could have wanted in life.

Two days later Kyle returned, alone. He stood on the porch after I opened the door and said nothing, he just stood there blinking. I remembered what Charlotte had predicted and guessed I knew what had happened but all I could think was how awful it was, how absolutely lonely he must be, to think that he would consider my house a refuge, and what a terrible person I must be to think he'd simply gotten what he deserved.

Gayle Hanratty

Goodwill

On the very morning we were to move into our new home, Joe died. He was in a rehab center recuperating from a stoke when a second assault swamped his fragile brain. He never awakened. A good way to go, they say—in your sleep. Forty-four years of ecstasy and anguish, of vulnerability and resilience—over in one pulsation.

I cancelled the move to the little yellow house in Louisville and instead buried myself in an old cottage tucked into the woods on the outskirts of Gray Hampton. The Sorry Cabin had been in our family for decades. It was Joe who'd dubbed it 'sorry,' given the shape it was in. Daughter Lilly and her partner Julien renovated the hidden-away shanty, adding rooms for Julien's children, Milo and Larken, and for themselves; they left the original cabin structure for Joe and me. It was where I thought we'd live out our decrepitude. But, once again life bequeathed its trickery, leaving me wallowing in sorrow over trusted and believed prospects—now moot.

Joe's unexpected demise has left me more than ragged—disconsolate and depressed. I've lapsed into mourning amongst the trees that watch over this sorriest of cabins—the place I also grieved over the death of our son, Ben.

I've been forcing myself to go to work with Lilly, at her behest, at the research forest a few days each week. Brambling through the mosses and arbors settles my trembling soul a mite—time's torment temporarily recedes. Time, not enough of it and yet too much, ticks and tocks on and on; one more imaginary notion that I cannot let go. How much of it do I have left? How do I fill the endless empty hours? These dichotomies are the same ones I suffered over when Ben died—the whys and the hows. The woods manage to take me out of my languor for an acorn's span.

Lilly and I stopped at a Goodwill store on the way home yesterday. She needed clothes suitable for crawling in the dirt. While she shopped, I cruised the store in a foggy ennui. I certainly didn't need clothes or dishes nor any more books. One item that caught my eye was a large glass enclosure resembling a greenhouse. It was a plant conservatory replica like you'd see at Kew Gardens in England or even at Eden Park in Cincinnati. I couldn't imagine why anyone would give away such a beautiful and unique showpiece. Although stained and dirty, all of the glass was intact and the wood foundation was lined with a copper tray. The price tag showed $35.00. I was intrigued. But, not in a buying mood, I left without giving it a home.

I cooked for myself most evenings to give Lilly and Julien time to themselves and their children. I have always cherished my time alone, as it seemed I could never get enough of it. And now alone time has mutated to loneliness. The anticipation of Joe's return from this place or that had staved off any lonesomeness and made seclusion precious. I understand now that the true enjoyment of solitude is actually in the expectation of connection.

After dinner, I trudged the woods around the Sorry Cabin inspecting the proliferation of mosses and cedar sprigs spreading and sprouting for dear life. Would these twigs and jade mats survive under glass—remembering the glass case I'd seen at Goodwill? I scooped up a clump of moss and uprooted two of the spindly three-inch cedars and brought them indoors. My cake plate and glass-dome lid made a fitting vessel in which to cultivate the flora. I used mulch from the humusy ground for a growing medium, snugged the plants in the dirt, then topped the container with the cover and placed it near a bright sunless north window.

A storm blew in that evening. Rain peppered the roof and lightning lit up the sky and the woods with quick spurts of daylight. The brilliant bursts illuminated the forest like the flashbulb of a camera, etching the scene like a snapshot.

Lilly and Julien allowed the Sorry grounds to grow naturally; they were not interested in grassy expanses or landscapes of ornamental bushes or shrubs. When trees fell, they'd let them lie as long as they didn't obstruct the way, then they'd plant an adolescent replacement in the resulting root crater. I imagined how my petite ecosystem might fare if I inserted miniature stumps and limbs. *What do you think, Joe?*

I peered into the forest-under-glass and was pleased by the way it mimicked the woods. Condensation formed dripping beads of dew on the plants like rain. The wee woodland charmed and distracted me. In the seventies terrariums were all the rage.

Rage lurked inside the wounded chambers of my heart and threatened to erupt at any affront. Though I kept it tamped and tamed neath a sober and somber veneer, I could sense its eagerness to flare. I knew I needed to harness and temper its fervor before it scorched my soul with its fiery tongues. Therapy would've been an option at fifty or even sixty, but at seventy such discourse seemed frivolous and inadequate. I'd been through this before and ought to know how to manage. At least, that's what I told myself. But now I needed sleep, even though it was usually fitful and brief, it was still a rest. The thought of a sweet, warm oatmeal breakfast gave me something to look forward to.

After my morning meal I heard Lilly knocking to see if I was ready to head out to the forest with her. I think she half expected me to decline her repeated invitations. But I was set to go—knapsack packed, walking stick in hand.

"Would you have any interest in dropping by the Goodwill again today? I saw something yesterday that I think I'll get."

"Of course, but why didn't you buy it yesterday?"

"I should have, but I was in no mood at the time."

"What is it?"

"I'll show you when we get there. If I tell you now, you might think I've gone thoroughly mad and refuse to stop."

"I doubt that, but okay; go ahead and be your enigmatic self."

Lilly parked in her assigned spot at work and headed off. "See you around 4:30, I'm eager to see your mysterious Goodwill treasure."

"Do you think I might be able to stroll through the propagation greenhouse and pinch a few plantlets?

"Sure, Mom, I'll let Clyde know you're pilfering. What are you going to do with them?"

"All in due time, dear. Patience!"

One of Lilly's responsibilities in the spring and summer months was to scour the forest for wildflowers. She photographed and mapped their locations and followed their progress over the years. She documented each species—Hepatica (buttercup), Cardamine (toothwort), Ranunculus (anemones), and Sanguinaria (bloodroot) were among her favorites. Many were common like trout lily and jewel weed, but she would purr with pleasure when she discovered a new or rare variety, like the Ginseng plant that is slowly being replaced by invasive vines and over-collected by herbalists. Of the research forest's 14,000 acres, only a few thousand are open to the public. Most of Lilly's research centered upon the non-public areas.

I gave Lilly a chance to talk with Clyde before I ventured to the propagation area. The planthouse was soggy with humidity and oppressive heat. I have always loved the feel of hothouse environments, like a toad cloaked by tall dewy grass, a sensation not dissimilar to relaxing in a sauna. If my job were to require me to toil in this atmosphere seven hours a day, my response may grow less agreeable.

Clyde was expecting me and waved me over when I entered. "What're you going to do with these cuttings Ms. Heddy, start your own nursery?"

"Sort of, but not really. I'm attempting to build terrariums, or is it terraria, and I want them to resemble the floor of the forest. Nothing complicated, just baby ferns or even creeping fig. Got anything like that?"

"Absolutely! I also have lots of hardy begonias. You can take as many of those as you want . . . Angel Wings, Dragon Wings, and plenty of the indoor type too."

I took all that he'd part with including a few spikey Aurelia and a Norfolk Pine. "Thanks Clyde, I'll let you know if they live. Oh, and I'd appreciate it if you didn't say anything to Lilly yet about the terrariums. She'll find out soon enough, but for now let's keep it between us."

"My lips are sealed Ms. Heddy."

I packed about twenty plants, each potted in one-inch clay, into a cardboard flat and stowed them in Lilly's Land Rover. Afterward, when I traipsed the woods, I observed the realm with fresh eyes. Before, I had peered forward or upward at the canopy or at the terrain ahead of me. Now, my view was fixed on the ground—on roots and mulchy leaves, on mosses, lichen, and tree mushrooms that I've always called 'puck.' I was tempted to poach a smidgen of this and a morsel of that, which I knew would go unnoticed by guests and rangers, but the golden rule for forest visitors was to 'take only pictures and leave only footprints.' The other reason I restrained from swiping vegetation was because I knew I could likely find all these items in my own woods at the Sorry Cabin. So, I trotted out my new Canon digital camera and zoomed in on the land.

What a day! I had spent seven full hours engrossed in something besides myself or Joe or Ben. After pity bingeing last night, I assumed today would be like every other since the living Joe became the late Joe. Once again, the woods had come to my rescue if only for this flickering moment.

I was waiting by the Land Rover when a golf cart trolleyed Lilly to her car. It wasn't as though she rode around in it all day. The vehicle delivered her to the far edges of the woods where she, then, walked or crawled in search of floral gold during the balance of her shady tenure.

She unfolded from the cart, grabbed her pack and arched backward with her hands at the base of her spine as though she'd spied a shrieky hawk. At forty, she was plenty young enough to scuttle around the earth on her knees or rump. But when you clamber about all day like that, even young bodies suffer and stiffen a bit.

When we arrived at the Goodwill store, I bolted out of the car, eager for my ensuing acquisition. Lilly followed me to the section where I had seen the case. The previous night I'd looked up 'miniature plant conservatory' on the Internet and found out that the enclosure was called a Wardian case. I walked circles around the table on which my hoped-for treasure had sat, but the case was gone.

"Well, they sold it. I should've bought it yesterday. Let's go."

"Ma'am, are you looking for that glass house that was on this table?" The young red-haired store clerk asked.

"Yes, I am. Looks like you sold it."

"Actually, one of our volunteers is cleaning it. He's almost finished. Do you still want it?"

"I do!" I was relieved that it had not sold.

"Glass house? What are we buying mom?"

I paid the clerk at the checkout counter and the volunteer carried my pearl of a purchase to the car.

"No thanks," he said, refusing my $5.00 tip.

There was something familiar about the volunteer's face and his voice. He had a manner about him that was eerily jarring. I gauged him older than me, but then I thought all people my age were older until I caught my own face in a mirror. I surmised he was likely a distant relative—a Skinner, Barkley, or Craycroft.

"What a cool find. So, this is why you wanted the plants."

"I want to make a few terrariums to dress up the cottage. I made one last night with scrapings from the woods. I'll show you when we get home. Did that volunteer look familiar to you? He creeped me out."

I visited with Lilly's family for an hour or so before going to my private quarters to eat dinner. Lilly ladled a bowl of soup and asked me to stay and eat with them, but I preferred eating alone tonight. As I fluttered my goodbyes, I told Lilly I wouldn't be joining her at work on Thursday.

"Okay mom, I'll stop by tomorrow morning before I leave."

Give out from a full day in the woods, I decided to wait until tomorrow to tackle the new terrarium. The one I'd made the previous evening was steamy with condensation. I lifted the lid and smelled the sweet dankness. It was the same scent that had flooded my faculties the day that Ben had been killed by a falling Ash tree. I brushed leaves and mulch just like this from his face and hair while we waited for the paramedics to arrive.

I got right to it on Thursday morning after breakfast. Even though the bristly man at Goodwill had dusted the loose dirt off the Wardian, I gave it a thorough cleaning, cluttering my counter with rags, Windex for the glass, and Bartenders' Friend for the copper pan. The terrarium stood eighteen inches high and was two feet square. There would be lots of room for plants.

Lilly offered to help me spade tufts of moss from the woods before she hustled off to work. We spooned sheet moss, cushion moss, and rock cap from the loamy turf, all in verdant splendor from the recent rains. In addition to moss, we collected clusters of bark and tree mushrooms.

"I could take the day off and help you with this, it looks like fun."

"Well, maybe you could help me on the weekend. I'd like to try this solo to start."

The terrarium consisted of three parts—the base, a box of glass panes framed in metal, and a rounded lid that was crowned with a bird. I coated the bottom with pebbles for drainage and added potting soil in uneven mounds and valleys. The tall Norfolk pine was the first to get planted. I arranged the ferns, begonias, and creeping fig beneath the pine's branches. The mosses and bark scattered around the rooted plants gave the terrarium a genuine appearance.

Joe and I had scavenged dozens of rocks and geodes ranging from pigeon to ostrich egg size off beaches and creeks we'd waded over the last half-century. The rocks would now occupy a proper venue inside the organic woodsy setting; no longer strewn along windowsills or serving as substitute paperweights. The stones paid tribute to our journey and thusly bestowed significance on the crafted bracken and brush, affording the terrarium character and soul.

Even though three months had passed since Joe's fatal attack, I led him on a tour of the conservatory, pointing out each nugget and reminding him of the excursion on which it had been purloined. The sound of his throaty chortling echoing in my head made me consider he might appreciate my latest harebrained venture. His imagined cackles have left me smiling—not weepy—a good sign, I think.

The Wardian case terrarium prospered over the next weeks. The more the vines filled in, the more it imitated the real forest. Milo and Larken became hypnotized by it and asked if they could add live skinks or toads. “The poor creatures wouldn’t make it,” I said, “they need bugs to eat and more sufficient ventilation to live.”

I began haunting Goodwill stores. Not just the one where I’d bought the Wardian; I preyed upon every market in and around Louisville. People donated valuable items to these second-hand stores that they could’ve sold on Ebay or at auction. In addition to glass, I bought shelving to hold the ground litter, pebbles, potting soil, and variety of vessels and lids I’d purchased.

I often chatted with Joe while constructing the earthy habitats. *I have a confession, Joe. I’ve become a terrarist. You should be worried; I might just dump thimblefuls of your ashes in each container.*

My portion of the Sorry Cabin became so cluttered with the menagerie of glass and greenery that Lilly grew concerned for my safety during nightly ventures through the darkened rooms. I assured her of my ability to flip light switches, but she remained skeptical.

“I have a suggestion and an offer for you. I spoke with our director about your penchant for making terrariums and described your limited studio space. And since your designs are in utter congruence with the conservancy of our culture, he proposed that you move your operations to the education center at the research forest. You’d occupy a corner of the main room with your own shelving and workbench, and you’d have easy access to water. And you could raid our greenhouses all you want, free of charge. Are you interested?”

“Do I have to pay rent?”

“In return, he asks that you chat with guests visiting the center and explain how a terrarium works. And maybe, if you felt so inclined, you could schedule a class or demonstration for our members.”

Lilly was giddy with expectation that I’d accept the generous offer, yet I was consumed with doubt over my ability or disability to relate to the public.

“I might be able to do that. Let me think on it a while.”

“Well, here’s the clincher,” Her eyes twinkled like lightning bugs on an August night. “You can even place your finished products in the Gift Shop on consignment. The store would keep fifty percent and you’d get the other half.”

“Hmm, it’d be a way to support my habit. I’ll ponder it for a day or so.

Lilly knew when to back off. She'd said her piece and it was in my lap now. Only a fool would reject such a win-win solution to my over-crowding of terrariums coupled with my need to continue to create them. But . . . I loved working in private, in peace and quiet. I've never been gregarious and the prospects of articulating my techniques with others made me nervous.

What do you think, Joe? Am I up to conversation and demonstration? I understood his answer when I rose from the couch and stumbled on the rug. My elbow clipped a cloche that domed one of the terrariums crashing it on the floor. I swept glass and dirt and fragile plants for twenty minutes. It was one of my favorites, dammit.

I drove the Volvo to the Goodwill nearest the research forest to search for new containers. That same volunteer was almost always there. Today he asked my name. I was taken aback by his question and gave him a sideways glance.

"If I have your name and phone number, I'd be happy to call you if someone drops off an interesting jar. That seems to be all you buy. Last week someone donated one of those large cases like you bought before, but it sold before you shopped again. If I knew you were going buy it, I could hold it for you." He seemed harmless enough now that his eyes had lost that jagged look that threatened to wound me if I got too close to him.

I wrote down my name and phone number on the back of a sales slip and handed it over.

"Heddy Carson." He read my name out loud. "I went to high school with a girl named Heddy, different last name though."

"No kidding! That's quite a coincidence. I would love it if you could keep your eye out for some interesting glass pieces. I like the bigger ones." I headed for the display shelves without asking his name. I found three items suitable for planting. Experience had taught me that larger environments sustained the greenery longer than the smaller ones. Cuttings were less likely to outgrow their habitat and their roots could stretch and spread in the wider confines.

I picked up a stack of glass plates for makeshift lids and an oversized bunch of resin grapes. These clusters of ornamental fruit had been popular in the fifties and sixties. With the adults of that generation now dying off, their heirs couldn't get rid of them fast enough. I bought all I could find. At home, I disassembled the clumps into individual orbs and glued them to improvised plate lids and candle stands, or I nestled them inside the growing area to resemble gazing balls.

Each time I purchased containers, my mind would start planning their transformation. I used acorn cupules for birds' nests or sprinkled dots of blue beads in the oaken hats for a birdbath.

I unloaded my non-heirlooms and wedged them on to the jam-packed worktable. He'd said he knew a 'Heddy' in high school. I never liked thinking about those years as it had not been a pleasant era for me. I was shy and lacking in conversational skills, which caused me to have a difficult time fitting in. I had girlfriends to run with and a few boyfriends to date, but nothing like the popular girls. I fared better in university where it was not so cliquish and competitive. Of course, it helped that it was an all-girls' college.

I thought it odd that the Goodwill volunteer had known a 'Heddy,' when I'd never met another. My father gave me the odd name before he died, before he even knew I was on the way. Hedwig Byrd was my great grandmother's name and Ivan, my father, mentioned to my mother that if they ever had another girl, he'd like to name her 'Heddy.' My sisters had normal names—Nicole is the oldest and Penny is in the middle. Ivan Barkley fell at a construction site in Louisville where he was a carpenter and died at the scene. Sal was two months pregnant with me and hadn't told him before he perished.

I poured a glass of wine and reached for a glass to pour a second one for Joe. Catching my slip, I replaced the glass and began reminiscing about the time Joe had visited me in the Sorry Cabin where I had hermitted myself for months. I was able to heal from our son's death within these walls because Joe was willing to be father and mother to Lilly.

I thought about how that volunteer's voice and demeanor had rankled me the first time I saw him. There was a familiar cadence and brusqueness that repelled me. His spikey manner was off putting, forewarning of danger. Since I assumed he was older than me, I thought it most unlikely that we'd gone to high school together. Yet it seemed even less likely that he knew another 'Heddy.'

I'd told Lilly I'd give her an answer about moving my hobby accouterments to the education center. I knew I had to give it a try, if for no other reason than safety. My work had become more than a hobby, like an obsession or a passion, I couldn't just give it up.

"I'll do it." I told her, though not totally convinced I could pull it off.

"We discussed the possibility of your setting up shop in the ed. center at the staff meeting and I showed photos of some of your creations. Everyone was enthusiastic about your terrariums, their artfulness and authenticity, as well as selling them in the gift shop. Everyone sees it as a perfect fit." Lilly had become my biggest cheerleader.

The next Saturday we loaded her Land Rover and Julien's pick-up truck with plastic tubs filled with glass containers, dirt, rock, bark, tools, and every last terrarium item that littered my cabin. I kept the domed cake plate and Wardian case as they were my first attempts as I liked how they warmed my modest abode. Everything else went, including the shelving units.

We seated twelve terrariums in the gift shop, rounded platters topped with cloches, tall apothecary jars, re-purposed fishbowls, and sealed glass canisters. Shelly, the gift store manager was gracious in accepting the consigned items. "These'll be gone in a month. You can bet on it."

After we unloaded Julien's truck, I asked Lilly and Jules if they would mind leaving me the Land Rover for the afternoon. I wanted to take my time arranging the paraphernalia, and I didn't want to feel harried or rushed by their helpful suggestions. They agreed and I went to the task of making a home, if only a corner, for my endeavors.

The space assigned was directly in front of a window out of which I could enjoy the arbors, meadows, and ponds on the grounds. I situated the workbench perpendicular to the window so I faced the entrance. The front doors were almost twenty-five feet away, but I could see who was coming or going.

As I was finishing up, my phone tootled. "Heddy here." I answered.

On the other end a man's voice barked, "Yes, hello Ms. Heddy, this is Vince Daniels from the Goodwill store. One of our regular donors has just dropped off one of those Wardian cases you like. It's not as big as the last one, but it's quite nice. Want me to hold on to it for you?"

My lungs were paralyzed, respirations halted. I retracted my diaphragm to draw in air and contracted it to push breath out. I couldn't faint right here, there were visitors wandering the center. I sat down on my work stool and steadied myself.

"Hello? Are you there?"

"Yes, yes," came out in a convulsive cough. "I'll be there in an hour."

I was unable to maintain any sane composure, so I made a beeline for the Land Rover where I could scream or pass out without an audience. There was no mistaking his name, Vince Daniels. I now knew why he was so recognizable. He'd known a 'Heddy' in high school all right.

We both went to Gray Hampton High School—Go Otters!

Vince Daniels and I hadn't just gone to the same high school, we were in the same class, and we were a couple. I wondered if Vince had already figured out the connection, when he asked for my name and number. I hadn't reciprocated with a similar request of his name, so this was the first I'd put two and two together.

I remained in the car the entire hour before proceeding to Goodwill, and phoned Lilly to say I would be late, advising her not to worry. I gave no explanation, but Lilly was used to my cryptic nature.

The only way I could calm myself was in conversation with Joe. *This is so weird, honey, you'd best sit down. I'm on my way to Goodwill to buy a terrarium container that the volunteer I told you about has sequestered for me. It has come to light in just the last hour that I know the man. He was my boyfriend in high school. Yes, the one you know about. How do I handle this? Give me a sign, anything.*

In the Goodwill parking lot, I lurked inside the parked Rover for another five minutes waiting for any hint of a response from Joe. When my hand touched the handle to open the car door, a voice inside me said *if you haven't told anyone, don't.* It wasn't Joe speaking; instead, it was the rasp of the crone who'd aborted the fetus I was carrying when I was sixteen. Of all people, I thought . . .

Teenage Vince had pleaded with me to 'go all the way.' I declined his appeals for months, but fearing he would break up with me if I denied his advances any longer, I gave in. It left me feeling pressured and used. Vince dumped me anyway, for a more popular and experienced girl. I'd never told anyone about the pregnancy or resulting abortion besides Joe.

Vince was at the counter with the Wardian case marked 'sold.' He was flapping the dust off it with a rag. He grinned as I approached.

"Vince Daniels, I thought you looked familiar. How long have you known who I was?"

"I recognized you the minute you sashayed through that door six months ago. Same confident walk and same green eyes. You haven't changed all that much. I've just been waiting for the proper opening to talk to you. My shift ended half an hour ago; want to walk across the street for a drink or a coffee? We can catch up on the last fifty-some-odd years."

I wasn't sure it was a good idea, but I also knew I had the upper hand, as I had Joe Carson inside me for guidance. "Okay, but just for a while. I'm driving my daughter's car and she may need it." A lie, but a convenient way out, if needed.

The bistro was friendly and bright. I ordered a Pinot Gris and Vince asked for a Stella.

"Did you marry? Got any kids? What type of work have you done all these years?"

"Slow up now, I want to hear about you. Obviously, you married—someone named Carson? And you have a daughter."

This is how the conversation went for a good hour. Vince had actually been the Executive Director of Goodwill Industries of Kentucky for thirty years. He retired when his wife became ill and subsequently died from cancer. After her death, he needed to keep busy, so that's when he began his volunteer stint at the Goodwill store.

I told him about Joe and about Ben and about Lilly's work at the research forest. I filled him in on my terrarium obsession and the move to the education center.

"I'll keep looking for those containers for you."

"Thanks Vince, that'd be nice. I ought to head home, it's a half-hour drive and it's getting dark." I opened my bag and offered to pay.

"I've got this, Heddy." By the way he looked out of the top of his eyes, I could see there was more he wanted to say. "Listen, I want to apologize for the way I treated you in high school. I shoved you aside like a sack of garbage. I was a jerk of the worst kind and a hormonal jerk at that. I have regretted my behavior the whole of my life. I am so thankful that I have the chance to tell you in person how sorry I am."

I broke the interminable silence that followed his penitent speech. "Well Vince, this has been quite an unexpected surprise. Your honesty and candor is commendable. Apology accepted. Now I really must make my way back to Gray Hampton. You should drop by the gift shop or the education center sometime and see what these containers have turned into."

I rambled on trying to break the edgy mood, sensing he wanted to continue the retrospection. I had to get away from him before I spilled my guts about the devastating circumstances of our teenage liaison that he never knew.

I pulled the Rover into the Sorry Cabin's driveway and ran inside for sanctuary. The weather had chilled. Another glass of wine and a blazing fire helped warm and relax me.

Remember how angry you were with me when I confessed to you about the abortion? You literally accused me of murder. We got through it; though you never quite forgave me. Anytime I go to that Goodwill now, I'll be reminded of my youthful failings and of that overwhelming period of my life.

My first day as a fixture in the center was on Tuesday. With school in session, only a few adult visitors wandered through. A couple stopped at my table.

"How interesting," the woman said. "So natural and peaceful. Are they difficult to maintain?"

"Not at all. Just give them light and let nature do the rest."

"Just water it occasionally?"

"No watering. Light causes condensation to form and they take care of themselves. There are several for sale in the gift shop."

An hour or so later, I looked up from my table and saw Vince ambling through the doors carrying a large round glass bowl. He was tall and still skinny and his thick black hair was now a tousle of gray curls. Khakis and flannel shirts were his clothing of choice and he wore Birkenstock sandals with socks.

"I went by the gift shop first." He said as he approached my station. "I'm not much of a plant person, but I can appreciate art when I see it. You've got quite a knack for this. Oh, this bowl came in this morning, can you use it?"

"Thanks Vince. It's perfect. How much do I owe you?"

"Five dollars," he said. "Mind you, I never meant to make you uncomfortable the other night. I just needed to get that off my chest."

"It's fine. I don't like being reminded of my high school years. Those were angst-filled times that I'd just as soon let lie."

"So, I guess if I asked you out to dinner, you wouldn't be interested."

"I don't know Vince. Joe hasn't even been gone a year. If feels a bit like a betrayal."

"It's only dinner, Heddy. I'm not asking you to marry me. There's a new place in downtown Louisville called Verona that I'd like to try out. We could meet there for an early dinner. How about Thursday at five?"

It seemed as though he'd been thinking about this as he had the time and place all planned out.

"I suppose dinner wouldn't hurt." I was glad he hadn't wanted to pick me up and that he expected me to pay for the bowl; it showed he respected my independence.

Two terrariums had sold by the end of the day on Thursday. It was reaffirming to know that people actually wanted them in their homes. It fueled my fervor to make more. At four-thirty I headed for downtown Louisville.

What am I doing Joe? Should I phone him and cancel? I'm not looking for companionship, so why did I accept his invitation? Plus, he's too much of a reminder of my misspent youth. It feels like I'm going backward, when all other aspects of my life are about growing and moving forward.

Vince was already seated and had selected a bottle of Pinot Grigio for us to share. He wore a corduroy sport coat and jeans, plus his customary flannel shirt and Birkenstocks. All through dinner, as I ate my eggplant Parmesan and Vince his veal, we reminisced about teachers and fellow students, wondering who of them remained among the living and which ones had passed.

"Do you remember how we all cruised for hours between the Dairy Dip and Jerry's. Those of us with cars were in a constant loop to meet up with our friends." He asked if I remembered his turquoise '57 Chevy. "I still have it in my garage. I'll probably give it to my grandson when he's old enough to drive."

"I do. I rode in that car many times."

Once the plates were cleared, the server poured the remainder of the Pinot into each of our glasses.

Vince raised his glass for a toast. "To many more dinners to come."

I lowered my glass without clinking his. "There aren't going to be any more dinners, Vince. This has been fun and I'm flattered by your attentions."

"I'm sensing a very large *but* here." Vince interrupted, looking embarrassed.

"But I'm not looking for a companion. Besides, all these ruminations through the halls of Gray Hampton High makes my stomach churn. I like my life the way it is Vince, no reflection on you. I'm just a crotchety old lady who wants to make terrariums."

"I understand Heddy. I don't like it, but I do understand. I hoped something might come of us, but I guess it's not in the oatmeal."

He handed the server his credit card, insisting on paying for dinner. "May I walk you to your car?" He asked touching my elbow.

"Of course." I'd parked close to the restaurant, so the mirthless march didn't last too long.

"Thanks for dinner, Vince."

"So long, Heddy." He actually saluted as he walked away.

I waited a couple weeks before I set foot in Vince's Goodwill store again. I shopped in skittish apprehension that he'd pop up from the behind a counter or shelf. I asked the clerk if it was his day off and she said he'd transferred his services to the St. Matthews store. "We were surprised because he'd made so many friends here, yourself included."

"I know you'll miss him." And they would, he was a dedicated helper. I, on the other hand was happy that I would not be bumping into him. It was a relief to know I could shop there in peace.

Not every terrarium sold in the weeks promised, two remained. Their sale further inspired me to continue my efforts. I was able to handle the limited conversations with center visitors better than I had anticipated; though I wasn't sure I'd ever get to the stage of offering a class or demonstration. It ended up that I kept a limited workshop at home. Since I only went to the center three or four days a week, I wanted to respond if the inspiration hit me.

I'm glad I didn't tell Vince he'd gotten me pregnant, or how I handled the situation. If I spurned his advances out of fear that he'd dump me again or that he'd die or even that he'd replace you, Joe, well, so be it. It's better this way with just you and me and my obsession.

Goodwill and the ed. center have prevented me from becoming the total recluse I was edging toward. It's approaching a year since Joe died and I've gotten over the abandonment and the deep, deep sorrow. And even though I still crave his company, Joe's presence is palpable in the woods and in each terrarium I plant, where growth flourishes and no sons or husbands die.

Editor's Note: While Gayle Hanratty's "Goodwill" stands here as an independent story, it can also be read as the final fiction in her book *Gray Hampton, A Suite of Stories,* published by *TLR*'s Fleur-de-Lis Press, 2017. Please see the back cover of this issue.

Cornerstone

work by writers K-12

Dana Serea

Girl Swimmer

I'm trapped underwater. My head is in chains,
muscles in pain, colorblind.

My arms overreach, my scent is bleach.
It's cold.

In the middle of the summer, I'm stranded in winter
with a splinter in my ear.

I'm a zombie. Skin dried,
hair fried, always hungry.

Then I'm back to the grind,
black line glued to my mind,

drowning helplessly, fighting an army,
fighting myself,

flipping and flapping, breaking and turning
in circles that never end.

I'm alone.
But out there, out of air, I'm breathing.

And when I go with it,
and flow with it,

I listen to the rhythm and find my faith,
and I'm not confined—I'm free.

I'm a wizard with toes on skipping stones,
my soul in celestial zones.

I dance upstream and dream the supreme:
effortless fire, working out and working in.

'Cause others may fear the deep,
but this girl is here to beat it.

Cindy Chen

The Life of a Swan

When the music echoed in the empty space,
I remember that I'm still flying.
Not for long, just a few meters on the stage.

Grand jeté, tendu, arabesque, I dulcified the lake's surface.
Preparing for the first play, I was young and blooming
when the music echoed in the empty space.

My arms—my wings—glided across the air with grace.
In the end, I bathed in claps and cheers, standing
not for long, just a few meters on the stage.

I've died, for a lifetime, in Swan Lake.
But even death, does not scare me as forgetting
when the music echoed in the empty space.

I consigned, inch by inch, to oblivion: the ballet, the *pas de deux*,
    the face
of my mother, name of my child. Even, my flying—
not for long, just a few meters on the stage.

My feathers, my flesh, my bones! Look how they made
weak in my old age! But oh, my heart! My heart is still reverberating!
When the music echoed in the empty space,
not for long, just a few meters on the stage.

Sophia Y. Zhang

Passion

Hold on to your passion,
For if it flies away,
You'll never feel determination
For day after day.

Hold onto your passion,
For if it is to fade,
You won't stand out with distinction.
You'll be sitting in a shade.

Mary Shea Ballantine

Melting Away

Have I ever told you about when I met your grandmother?
I was at a play, laughing loudly.
She tapped me on the shoulder and shushed me,
But she was the most gorgeous lady I'd ever seen,
So I asked her to sit next to me.

Her name was Marie, she said.
We went to the stores across 5th Street that night—talking nonstop.
We carried on for two years, and then we had your wonderful mother,
Grace.
She lit up Marie's eyes when she'd dance and hop around.
What a little dancer.
I see her in you all the time.

Do you want to hear about how I met my—I mean your—grandma?
I was at an opera, singing along, but she got upset.
She shushed me, but I couldn't let her sit back down alone.
I sat next to her.

She introduced herself as Mary.
That night we all went down 5th Street.
Then we had a daughter named Grey.
She became a dancer—or no, she just loved to dance.
And soon she had a daughter—you!
Right?

I'm gonna tell you how I met someone—my best friend.
I went down to a theatre, and fell asleep.
I woke up next to a gorgeous woman.

Molly was her name.
We sat in the cinema, no, theatre, and talked forever.

We met up again and again.
She had a child. The baby was a girl.
I loved that baby—what happened to it?
Do you know?
Someone else had a baby, Gabby, or something like that, was it?
Their baby looked like mine—are you my child?

I met a girl at the park—she was perfect.
It was Macy—no, no. Marley.
I like that Maria a lot.
That night she talked and met a child.
What was its name?
Where did they go?
Well, now you're here, and, um,
Wait, who are your parents?
Grace, ah.
I knew a dancer named Gracie . . . she was good.
Pretty, like a woman I met in a theatre . . .

Andy Li

I Am a Leaf

I am as green as fresh grass.
I twist in the air as I try with all my might to stay on the branch as
a boy pulls me away.
I see the boy reaching for a flower instead.
I hear the whistling of the wind soften, as night settles back down.

Yunzhong Mao

New Year

The moon is shining tonight.
It slowly drifts in the sky.
The light pours on the street,
cascading as a waterfall

It penetrates one's mind
and impales one's heart.
Emitting the inescapable shrieking sound
of a war prisoner being tortured, and tortured

The crippled beggar plods across the sidewalk,
and peeks inside a restaurant where the feast commences.
He stands there, numb expression on his face
Ignored by the world, human litter tossed upon the road

The old lady stands in front of the grave
of her veteran son who died in the war
body washed away by the sea, lost
She kneels and sobs as cars speed by

Happy new year! Happy new year!
People chant like a chorus
but who really knows what new year means
Who really knows, who really knows?

Julia Multer

Basement

Plastic plates caked with dry paint. Windows drawn closed
in early evening. The crackle of the second-hand radio

as the only sound in the basement. Brush he twirls in his fingers.
Shy glances serve as conversation that we dismiss as simple friendliness.

Understanding that this is a room without judgement. Understanding
when he brings the color to the canvas in a splash of red,

and conversation serves as a filler. He watches his work,
shallow breathing. A cluttered desk. An artist's sanctuary
    transformed into

a confession booth. He tells me not to stand so close, and I,
embarrassed, retreat to watch from afar.

Audrey Kim

Think of Me in the Presence Tense

Is it Spring now, where you are
Flowers blossom into the brightest occasions
There were dozens: rouge reds, blush pinks on
The river bank that spooned the meadow
We used to visit. Knees deep in tall grass;
Standing, facing each other;
Zinnias protruding from our irises,
Petulance in the petals of our palms

Hot red heels plunging into the soil like stakes;
You never liked when I wore those shoes.
And I hated the way you folded
Your arms in reproach, scowling as I flounced
Through the California poppies. Critical
Of my *disregard for life* to which I say

Think of me in the presence tense
Find my face in red skies that tear across summer
Nights. Whisper my name at the convenience
Store. Savor the sting of sour lemonade.
Likewise, I'll seek the smoke that settles outside bars
And remember the musk of your chest, until the whiskey
Runs warm down my throat, and soil grows
Between the canyons of my spine.

Notes on Contributors

Susan Ayres is a poet, lawyer, and translator. She holds an MFA in creative writing with a concentration in translation from Vermont College of Fine Arts, and a PhD in literature from Texas Christian University. Her work has been nominated for a Pushcart Prize, and has appeared in many journals, including *Sycamore Review, Cimarron Review, Valparaiso Review.* She lives in Fort Worth and teaches at Texas A&M University School of Law. She can be reached at https://psusanayres.com/. The translated poem "Song," included in this issue is from the longer poem by Elsa Cross, "Galaxidi."

Claudia Buckholts received Creative Writing Fellowships from the National Endowment for the Arts and Massachusetts Artists Foundation, and the Grolier Poetry Prize. Her work has appeared in *Indiana Review, Minnesota Review, New American Writing, Prairie Schooner, The Southern Review, Tar River Poetry,* and others; and in two books, *Bitterwater* and *Traveling Through the Body.*

Christopher Buckley's recent books are *Agnostic* (Lynx House Press, 2019) and *The Pre-Eternity of the World* (Stephen F. Austin State Univ. Press 2021). He has recently edited: *The Long Embrace: Contemporary Poets on the Long Poems of Philip Levine,* (Lynx House Press, 2020); and *Naming the Lost: The Fresno Poets—Interviews & Essays,* (Stephen F. Austin State Univ. Press, 2021). He is a previous contributor to *TLR.*

Kelly Craig is an emerging writer from Salt Lake City, Utah. She is a PhD Candidate in Literary and Cultural Studies, and her fiction and creative nonfiction has appeared in *Litro Magazine, Golden Walkman Magazine, Sakura Review*, and elsewhere.

Elsa Cross (Mexico City, 1946) is a poet, critic, and translator. She holds a professorship in the National Autonomous University of Mexico, where she teaches philosophy of religion. She has been awarded the National Prize of Arts and Literature, the highest literary award in Mexico, and she has received many other poetry prizes in Mexico, as well as Canada, France, Switzerland, and Italy. Fourteen of her poetry collections have been translated and published in different countries. Many of her books have been inspired by her stays in India and Greece, and by travels throughout her own country. The poem, "Cancíon," included in this issue is from the longer poem, "Galaxidi."

Olga-Maria Cruz (she/her/hers) is a poet and essayist whose work has appeared in journals including *Poetry East, Carolina Quarterly, and Bellevue Literary Review*, and anthologies by Lee Gutkind (*Same Time Next Week*, In Fact Books) and Erin Keane's *The Louisville Anthology* (Belt Publishing 2020). She currently serves as the Lutheran campus minister to Winthrop University.

Angela D'Ambra achieved a specialized degree in Foreign Languages and Literatures from the University of Florence (2008); a Master II degree in translation of post-colonial texts from English into Italian at the University of Pisa (2009). Since 2010 she has been translating non-profit poetic texts. Her translations have been published in various Italian online and printed magazines. For IMPREMIX she edited and translated the first three volumes of a series dedicated to Canadian poetry. For Efesto she translated (pro bono) Abhay K.'s book, *The Alphabets of Latin America*. For Puntoacapo Editore, *Giacomo: Opera of a Solitaire,* by David Cappella.

Vicki Derderian is a fiction writer living in Chapel Hill, North Carolina. Her work has been published in the *Michigan Quarterly Review, Independence Boulevard, Ararat,* and the *London Reader.*

Andrea Doll is a Louisville, Kentucky native who is currently studying English and Psychology at Bellarmine University.

Patricia Foster is the author of *All the Lost Girls* (PEN/Jerard Award), *Just beneath My Skin* (essays), *Girl from Soldier Creek* (SFA Novel Award) and the editor of four anthologies, most recently, *Understanding the Essay* (with Jeff Porter). She received a Pushcart Prize, a Clarence Cason Award, a Theodore Hoepfner Award, a Dean's Scholar Award, a Yaddo Fellowship, and other awards, and has been a professor in the MFA Program in Nonfiction at the University of Iowa for over twenty-three years. She also taught writing in France, Australia, Italy, Czech Republic, and Spain.

Sarah Gorham is a poet and essayist, and most recently the author of *Alpine Apprentice* (2017), which made the short list for 2018 PEN/Diamonstein Award in the Essay and Study in Perfect (2014), selected by Bernard Cooper for the 2013 AWP Award in Creative Nonfiction. Both were published by University of Georgia Press. Gorham is also the author of four collections of poetry—*Bad Daughter* (2011), *The Cure* (2003), *The Tension Zone* (1996), and *Don't Go Back to Sleep* (1989). Other honors include grants and fellowships from the National Endowment for the Arts and three state arts councils. She is co-founder and editor-in-chief at Sarabande Books, an independent, nonprofit, literary publisher, now celebrating its twenty-seventh anniversary.

Gayle Hanratty's short story collection *Gray Hampton* was published in 2017 by Fleur-de-Lis Press. Her short stories have appeared in *Monkscript, The Louisville Review*, and *Trajectory*, where she was co-winner of their inaugural short story contest. Gayle lives in Louisville with her husband, George. She is a graduate and retired staff member of Spalding University's Masters of Fine Arts in Wtiting Program.

A graduate of the University of Maryland, **C. B. Heinemann**'s stories have appeared in *Berkeley Review, Charitan Review, Florida English, Parhelion Literary Magazine, Press, Outside In Magazine, Danse Macabre, Rathalla Literary Review, Mountain Tales Press, Cigale Literary Review, Writers Who Rock, Biostories, Write Place At the Right Time, Ascent, Storyteller, The Battered Suitcase, Spilt Infinitives, Whistling Shade, Lowestoft Chronicles,*

Outside In Review, One Million Stories, and *Fate.* Heinemann has also written for *The Washington Post, Boston Globe, Philadelphia Inquirer,* and *Car & Travel.*

Marcia L. Hurlow is the author of a full-length poetry collection, *Anomie,* and five chapbooks. Her poems have appeared in more than 400 literary magazines, including *Poetry, Poetry Northwest, Stand, Chicago Review, Zone 3, Malahat Review* and *Poetry Wales.* She is co-editor of *Kansas City Voices.*

John James is the author of *The Milk Hours* (Milkweed, 2019), selected by Henri Cole for the Max Ritvo Poetry Prize. A PhD candidate in English at UC Berkeley, his poems appear in *Boston Review, Kenyon Review, Gulf Coast, PEN America, Best American Poetry,* and elsewhere.

Nicholas Korn is a poet, playwright and composer living in Cincinnati, OH. He started writing the *Wild Sonnets* in 2016, and the project now includes over 350 poems. For more information on this and other projects: www.nicholaskorn.com.

Sarah Landenwich is a novelist and poet who lives in Denver. She is currently at work on her debut novel, *The Fire Concerto.*

Nathan Alling Long has work on NPR and in over 100 publications, including *Tin House, Glimmer Train, Story Quarterly,* and *Witness.* His stories have won international contests and his collection of 50 short fictions, *The Origin of Doubt,* was a 2019 Lambda Literary Award finalist. Other awards include a Truman Capote Literary Scholarship, Mellon Foundation Fellowship, and scholarships to both Bread Loaf and Sewanee writers' conferences.

Neema Muneer is a perennial recluse living in Saudi Arabia with her husband and two children. She is currently working on her debut novel.

Kentucky poet, folklorist, educator, and naturalist **Sarah McCartt-Jackson**'s work has appeared in *Bellingham Review, Indiana Review, Journal of American Folklore, The Maine Review, Tidal Basin Review,* and others. She is the recipient of an Al Smith Individual Artist Fellowship from the Kentucky Arts Council, and has served as artist-in-residence for four National Parks: Great Smoky Mountains, Acadia, Catoctin Mountain National Park, and Homestead. She is the author of *Stonelight* (Airlie Press), which won the Phillip H. McMath Award, Weatherford Award in Poetry, and Airlie Prize. Her chapbooks include *Calf Canyon, Vein of Stone,* and *Children Born on the Wrong Side of the River.*

Jeff McLaughlin was born in Nebraska, grew up in the Carolinas, went to school in Minnesota, and now lives and works in Paris with his wife and two young children. He's been fortunate enough to place a few stories here and there, most notably in the *Kenyon Review Online* and *december* magazine and most recently in the *Sky Island Review* and the *Southern Humanities Review.* In between editing his first novel, he serves as a reader for the *Raleigh Review.*

While **Tony O'Keeffe** has published poetry in *The Louisville Review* before, "At the Concert" is his first published work of fiction.

Greg Pape is the author of *Four Swans, Animal Time, American Flamingo*, and several other books. He served as Montana Poet Laureate 2007 to 2009. Professor Emeritus at University of Montana, he teaches in the MFA program at Spalding University's Sena Jeter Naslund-Karen Mann Graduate School of Writing.

Erik Peters is a teacher from Vancouver, BC, Canada. Twice a graduate of the University of British Columbia, Erik has been published in a number of literary magazines. An avid mediaevalist, Erik can read Latin, Middle English, is conversationally fluent in Spanish and lives with his wife and three pet rats.

Lynne Potts has three books of poetry, two by National Poetry Review Press and one by Glass Lyre Press. Her work has appeared in *The Southern Review, Paris Review, The Literary Review, Yale Review, American Letters, California Quarterly*, and many others. Lynne has been the recipient of several awards including four fellowships. She was made a Massachusetts Cultural Council Fellow in 2012. She lives in Boston and New York.

Professor Emeritus of English at SUNY Orange, **J.R. Solonche** has published poetry in more than 500 magazines, journals, and anthologies since the early 70s, including *The New Criterion, The New York Times, The American Scholar, The Progressive, Poetry Northwest, Salmagundi, The Literary Review, The Sun, The American Journal of Poetry, Poet Lore, Poetry East, The Hampden-Sydney Poetry Review, The Journal of the American Medical Association,* and *Free Verse.* He is the author of *Beautiful Day* (Deerbrook Editions), *Won't Be Long* (Deerbrook Editions), *Heart's Content* (Five Oaks Press), *Invisible* (nominated for the Pulitzer Prize by Five Oaks Press), *The Black Birch* (Kelsay Books), *I, Emily Dickinson & Other Found Poems* (Deerbrook Editions), *In Short Order* (Kelsay Books), *Tomorrow, Today and Yesterday* (Deerbrook Editions), *True Enough* (Dos Madres Press), *The Jewish Dancing Master* (Ravenna Press), *If You Should See Me Walking on the Road* (Kelsay Books), In a Public Place (Dos Madres Press), *To Say the Least* (Dos Madres Press), *The Time of Your Life (*Adelaide Books), *The Porch Poems* (Deerbrook Editions, 2020 Shelf Unbound Notable Indie Book), *Enjoy Yourself* (Serving House Books), *Piano Music* (nominated for the Pulitzer Prize by Serving House Books), *For All I Know* (Kelsay Books), *A Guide of the Perplexed* (Serving House Books), *The Moon Is the Capital of the World* (WordTech Communications), *Years Later* (Adelaide Books), *The Dust* (Dos Madres Press), *Selected Poems 2002-2021* (nominated for the National Book Award by Serving House Books), and coauthor with his wife Joan I. Siegel of *Peach Girl: Poems for a Chinese Daughter* (Grayson Books). He lives in the Hudson Valley.

John Surowiecki is the author of thirteen books of poetry, most recently *Burger King of the Dead* (Grayson Books). Later in the year, Wolfson Press will publish his fourteenth book, *The Place of the Solitaires: Poems from Titles* by Wallace Stevens. He has also written a novel, *Pie Man*, which won the Nilsen Prize for a First Novel in 2017.

Jason Tandon is the author of four books of poetry, including *The Actual World* (Black Lawrence Press, 2019) and *Give Over the Heckler and Everyone Gets Hurt* (Black Lawrence Press, 2009), winner of the St. Lawrence Book Award for a first collection. His poems have appeared in *Ploughshares, Prairie Schooner, Beloit Poetry Journal, North American Review, Esquire,* and elsewhere. He is a senior lecturer in the Arts & Sciences Writing Program at Boston University.

Chelsie Taylor lives in central Kentucky, where she and her husband keep bees and plant pollinator habitat. She was most recently published in *Poetry East, Number 100: The Bliss of Reading.*

Maria Tori is a Japanese-American poet, painter, and bird lover. This will be her first published poem, hopefully of many. She resides in Louisville, Kentucky, where she lives with her beloved dog, Georgia, who reminds her to be authentic, curious, and assertive each day.

Seth Brady Tucker is the executive director of the Longleaf Writers' Conference at Seaside, Florida, and his essays, poems, and stories have appeared in such magazines and journals as *December, Iowa Review, Shenandoah, Poetry Northwest, Verse Daily, Blackbird, Birmingham Poetry Review,* and the *Los Angeles Review.*

Jonathan Weinert is the author of three books of poems: *A Slow Green Sleep*, winner of the Saturnalia Books Editors Prize; *In the Mode of Disappearance*, winner of the Nightboat Poetry Prize; and *Thirteen Small Apostrophes*, a chapbook. He is co-editor, with Kevin Prufer, of *Until Everything Is Continuous Again: American Poets on the Recent Work of W. S. Merwin.* "I Couldn't Say No" is an excerpt from his unpublished memoir, *Five Minutes in Heaven.*

Nadeem Zaman is the author of the novel *In the Time of the Others* (longlisted for the 2019 DSC Prize in South Asian Literature) and the story collection *Up in the Main House & Other Stories*. His fiction has appeared in *Singapore Unbound, Roanoke Review, The Wilderness House Literary Journal, Copperfield Review, Cha: An Asian Literary Journal, Dhaka Tribune, Dhaka Daily Star, Bengal Lights, 94 Creations*, and other journals. His novel *The Inheritors* is forthcoming in 2022.

Notes on Contributors to Cornerstone

Mary Shea Ballantine, 14, recently graduated from St. Francis of Assisi Catholic School and started Fall 2021 at Sacred Heart Academy in Louisville, Kentucky.

Cindy Chen is a high school senior at Culver Academies. She has been recognized by the Scholastic Art and Writing Awards and Kenyon Young Writers Workshop and is the editor in chief of the school's literary magazine. As a traveler and a daydreamer, she writes about her experience in both Chinese and western cultures and her wild imagination, including topics like Buddhism, social phenomenon, and her life as an international student. She is currently working on her autobiographical fiction *The Prophecy of Marek* with the help of coffee and dark chocolate.

Audrey Kim is a seventeen year old writer from Torrance, California. Her work appears in *Dear Asian Youth Literature*, *Overachiever Magazine*, and others. *The Goldfinch* is her favorite novel.

Andy Li (or You An Li in Chinese) is a 9-year-old student at Renaissance College in Hong Kong. From ages 5 to 9, he was a student at Hong Kong Academy. He loves fantasy stories. The poem "I Am a Leaf" was written when he was 8. Andy's first printed poem, "Spring," written a year earlier, appeared in *Stonesoup* in March 2021.

Yunzhong Mao is a high school sophomore born in Shanghai before moving to Massachusetts to experience different kinds of culture and obtain a more international outlook. Originally self-defined as an Astro Boy whose imagination soared exclusively over the sea of scientific equations, he soon discovered his hidden passion for reading and writing poems in this new land. His literary inspiration draws from a wide range of experiences such as music, films like *The Grand Budapest Hotel*, and people watching.

Julia Multer, a rising Senior at the Lycée Français de Chicago, has been published in *Hot Dish Magazine* (Award Winner Short Fiction), *elementia online magazine*, (1st place Short Story), and *Voices de la Luna* (poetry). She was one of 13 students selected nationally to participate in an intensive course in Creative Writing at Northwestern University under the professorship of poet Richie Hofmannhis culminated in her original chapbook entitled *Under These Tracks*, a collection of poetry inspired by the city of Chicago. She attended the School of the New York Times Summer Writing Academy in July of 2021.

Dana Serea is a rising senior at Rutherford High School in Rutherford, New Jersey. She loves competitive swimming, photography, and writing. Her work has been published in *Canvas Literary Journal*, *Lunch Ticket/School Lunch*, *Bluefire*, and in the *Poetry Society of Virginia* anthology. She is the winner of a Scholastic Art & Writing National Gold Medal, as well as a multiple Gold Key winner in the state of New Jersey for writing and photography. She won the 1st place in the 2020 Renée Duke Youth Award Poetry Contest for Human Rights for poetry, the 1st place in the 2020 Ringling College for Art and Design "Storytellers of Tomorrow" Writing Contest for a short story, as well as several third places and honorable mentions in national contests for her poetry and prose.

Sophia Yuxin Zhang was born in California in 2010 and resides in Utah with her beloved family, including her two young budgies, Cookie and Loki. Sophia is a chess player and swimmer. Besides literature, she also loves golfing and going on trips.

About the Front Cover Artist

Corie Neumayer, a painter in Louisville, Kentucky, works mainly in acrylic, latex, found papers, and aerosol. Her formative years were spent in the rural areas of Eastern Kentucky, and they continue to influence her work. She has spent much of her life teaching art to students in Indiana, California, and Louisville, Kentucky.

Her paintings are in public and private collections and she has shown regionally and nationally. Neumayer is a member of PYRO Gallery, and her work can be found there and at CorieNeumayerPaintings.com.

www.ingramcontent.com/pod-product-compliance
Lightning Source LLC
Chambersburg PA
CBHW032022050726
47590CB00006B/2270

* 9 7 8 0 5 7 8 3 2 7 9 6 9 *